Child Health Care
and the Working Mother

Child Health Care and the Working Mother

The juggling act

Jenny Hewison PhD
Senior Lecturer

and

Therese Dowswell PhD
Research Fellow
Department of Psychology
University of Leeds, UK

CHAPMAN & HALL
London · Glasgow · New York · Tokyo · Melbourne · Madras

Published by Chapman & Hall, 2–6 Boundary Row, London SE1 8HN

Chapman & Hall, 2–6 Boundary Row, London SE1 8HN, UK

Blackie Academic & Professional, Wester Cleddens Road, Bishopbriggs, Glasgow G64 2NZ, UK

Chapman & Hall Inc., 29 West 35th Street, New York NY10001, USA

Chapman & Hall Japan, Thomson Publishing Japan, Hirakawacho Nemoto Building, 6F, 1–7–11 Hirakawa-cho, Chiyoda-ku, Tokyo 102, Japan

Chapman & Hall Australia, Thomas Nelson Australia, 102 Dodds Street, South Melbourne, Victoria 3205, Australia

Chapman & Hall India, R. Seshadri, 32 Second Main Road, CIT East, Madras 600 035, India

Distributed in the USA and Canada by Singular Publishing Group Inc., 4284 41st Street, San Diego, California 92105

First edition 1994

© 1994 Chapman & Hall

Typeset in 10/12pt Palatino by Mews Photosetting, Beckenham, Kent
Printed in Great Britain at the University Press, Cambridge

ISBN 0 412 48320 3   1 56593 235 8 (USA)

A catalogue record for this book is available from the British Library

Library of Congress Cataloging-in-Publication data available

For Katie and Ellie, Alice and John

Contents

Acknowledgements

We would like to thank all the parents and all the school staff who helped us collect the information we needed for our research.

We would also wish to express our gratitude to the Economic and Social Research Council for providing the funds that made the study possible.

1

Introduction

This book is about the health care which families provide for children. Most of that health care is provided by mothers, as is most of child care in general. When mothers take on paid work, patterns of child care obviously change and a good deal has already been written about the problems which working mothers have in reconciling their family and employment responsibilities.

This book reports the findings of a research project which broke new ground in two main ways: it looked specifically at child health care, a potentially very fraught aspect of care; and it looked at the needs of school age children. The project tried to find out what factors were being taken into account by parents in the decision to keep a child home from school; and in particular, whether mothers in paid work made these kinds of decisions differently from mothers who were at home.

It is perhaps surprising that more is not known about this topic already, since every day millions of women are having to make decisions in which the health care needs of their children are being weighed against their employment obligations.

As always, there are problems when conflicting interests have to be reconciled. In ordinary life, these particular problems are largely invisible: family problems solved in private. This book is, in part, an attempt to make them public problems, because they have obvious relevance to current debates about women's employment, the development and well-being of children, the nature of the family and indeed the workings of the labour market within the national economy.

Official statistics indicate the scale of women's employment activity in the UK: in 1991, among women with a child under five, 43% were in employment (already quite a high value and a big increase on the 24% recorded in 1983), but among mothers with a youngest child between five and nine, this figure had risen to 67% (OPCS Monitor, 1992).

Thinking first about the under-fives, the provision of child care for this age group has been relatively well researched and reported. By contrast, virtually no attention has been paid to the difficulties women have in reconciling their family and employment obligations once their children have entered school. Further, while after-school and holiday care for school aged children can at least be planned in advance, childhood illness episodes are not only unpredictable but also almost inevitable and create quite a different set of problems. This book examines these problems and the ways mothers deal with them.

Most of the material in the chapters to follow comes from a research project conducted in the city of Leeds, in the north of England. All the families who took part in the study lived in stable, white, working class areas of the city and were recruited via the schools attended by their 6–7-year-old children. This is not, in other words, a book about 'dual career' families, by which we mean families where both parents follow well paid professional or managerial occupations. Such families are very rare in the UK and their needs and concerns are not necessarily relevant to those of the majority. The women described in this book are like millions of others who do clerical or manual jobs and who form overwhelmingly the greater part of the female workforce in the UK economy.

Chapter 2 provides a detailed description of the project in Leeds. The remainder of this introductory chapter attempts to provide a context for a study of parents' employment and child health care by outlining some of the main facts about 'the working woman' and the problems that she faces. The material presented is drawn from a very large literature and body of expertise spanning several academic disciplines, including economics, management studies, demography, sociology, social policy and women's studies. No attempt is made to be exhaustive or to throw new light on areas well worked by others; the purpose is rather to ensure that all readers of the chapters to follow are familiar with the social and economic context against which our own study findings must be interpreted.

WOMEN IN PAID WORK

The main facts are well known. Government statisticians report regularly on the numbers of women in paid work, on whether they are working full- or part-time and on basic demographic facts about them such as their age and whether or not they have children. All of this information is available for the main geographical regions of the country, as well as for the UK nationally.

The single central fact has already been mentioned: more and more women are joining the labour force. Other trends in the economy, such as the current recession, obscure the picture but the underlying trend is strongly upwards and women are expected to fill 90% of a projected increase of 1 million new jobs by the turn of the century (EOC, 1990). In the UK, as in other European countries, these changes increasingly involve mothers of dependent children.

It is almost superfluous to point out that most of these women have working lives very different from those of men. They are much more likely to spend periods of time out of the workforce, to work part-time and to work in less skilled and less well-paid jobs. The pay gap between women and men is almost as big as it was a decade ago: women earn less than men per hour and the disparity in income is greater still because men work much longer hours than women do. Fathers of under-fives in the UK work the longest hours in Europe, with more than a third working 50 hours a week or even longer. By contrast, the fulltime employment rate for mothers of under-fives is the second lowest in the European Community and for mothers of children aged five to nine, the third lowest.

There has been considerable speculation as to why part-time working for women should be such a feature of the UK economy. Is it because this is what British women prefer ('supply side factors' in the language of economics) or because of 'demand side factors' in the kinds of employment on offer to them? In a recent study of women's attitudes towards work

(Dex, 1988), emphasis is placed on the advantages to employers of taking on part-timers. National Insurance contributions payable by employers are smaller and employees have fewer benefits and contractual safeguards. These are not features of employment practice in other industrialized countries and the extent of part-time work seen there is much less in consequence. Supply side changes, for example in women's attitudes, were believed to have been contributory to the development of the British pattern, but on the whole to have been of lesser importance. The influence they did have tended to be indirect: more women wanted to work but also accepted that they retained primary responsibility for child care. As the report of this study pointed out, in these circumstances, 'Part-time employment has been therefore a reasonable solution'.

The position for men is more straightforward. As the author of the above report states, ' . . . attitude change amongst men to make them want to work fewer hours and give up the notion that they are fulltime breadwinners, has not been very extensive to date'. Since overtime working is also a feature of the British economy, it makes financial sense for men to work extra hours for high rates of pay, rather than for women to work the same number of hours at much lower rates of pay. This stalemate is unlikely to be easily broken, although the European Commission is trying to raise the issues as part of equal opportunity policies.

> If all types of jobs could be structured so that the hours norm for the job was a lot less than it is at present, with more opportunity for job sharing, but without the contractual and benefit losses that part-time work often involves, then a redistribution of work might begin to be possible, both within the household and between households.
>
> *(Dex, 1988)*

Nobody thinks this will be easy. Another finding from the work attitudes study, entirely consistent with basic psychological work on attitudes, is that employment experience influenced attitudes as well as the other way around. In other words, as women gained more work experience, they tended to exhibit fewer traditional attitudes to women's roles. Too much optimism is not justified, however, since for most women the work experience they are likely to get is heavily constrained by what economists call the sex segregation of labour markets. This does not just refer to the obvious fact that some jobs (school dinner lady) are almost universally filled by women while other jobs (dustman) include hardly any, but also that a whole class of jobs is fundamentally structured around the time availability of working mothers. Such jobs often have so little else to commend them that only people with limited choices will take them. This pattern then perpetuates the kind of stereotyping in which women and girls accept that some kinds of jobs are 'for them' and many, many more are not.

A recent report from the Equal Opportunities Commission (EOC, 1992) shows how much needs to be achieved in terms of pay. In 1984, legal changes were introduced allowing women to claim the same pay as a man doing a different job, if the two jobs could be shown to be of 'equal value'. This legislation has been of limited impact: eight years later, women's average hourly earnings are only 77% of men's and the figure is even smaller when weekly earnings are being considered, because of the huge difference in the number of hours worked.

The authors of the EOC report argue that market forces alone are unlikely to change matters very much since in the UK, as in most other countries, 'custom and practice', organizational structures and social values all exert powerful pressures in favour of the status quo. It could be added that, on the domestic stage, men's image of themselves as 'head of household' is in large part based on their control of financial resources. For most men, their partner would have to be very well paid before the overall increase in the size of the cake compensated for their own decreased share of it. Choices of this kind are open to very few families indeed. On the whole, women's bargaining position is weak, industry is always seeking to reduce its labour costs and female labour comes cheap.

Less obvious and hence less well known than the facts about pay rates, hours of work and the sex segregation of labour markets is the phenomenon of 'downward occupational mobility'. Women who begin their working lives in quite good jobs appropriate to their education and qualifications nonetheless tend to exhibit such downward mobility after having children; that is, they return to work in less responsible and less well paid jobs, often on a part-time basis (Brannen, 1989). The consequent loss of earnings can be very substantial: child bearing and child rearing have been estimated to cost the average UK mother of two more than half of her potential lifetime's earnings (Joshi, 1987).

Looked at simply from the needs of the economy, women's work patterns are obviously very wasteful. Talents and expensively acquired skills are not being used. Even in times of recession, when job selectors can easily fill their vacancies, they are necessarily recruiting from a reduced pool of talent and when the economy is expanding, skill shortages can be a major limiting factor in economic recovery.

Even though it is unclear when the present recession will end, labour shortages may well arise before then as a result of a phenomenon which has come to be known as 'the demographic time bomb'. As a result of a falling birthrate in the 1970s, the UK is now facing a pronounced decline in the number of young people entering the labour market. Between 1989 and 1995, the number of 16–19–year–olds is expected to fall by 23% or nearly 600 000, while the number of 16–24–year-olds is expected to drop by some 1.2 million. Attracting and retaining women workers have been widely hailed as the answer to this problem and Norman Fowler, whilst Secretary of State for Employment, dubbed the 1990s as 'the decade of the working woman'.

Before the current recession displaced the topic from the political and economic agenda, the special needs of working mothers began to receive some attention from policy makers. Lack of suitable and affordable child care was identified as the main barrier to increasing the number of women in the labour force and a number of minor policy changes were actually introduced, such as the tax advantages designed to encourage employers to provide workplace nurseries.

In introducing these changes, there was of course more than the economy to be considered. 'The Family' has always attracted a lot of attention from government and from the media, particularly when the explanation of social ills is being considered. Within the Conservative Party the issue of 'working mothers' and whether to encourage women to stay at home and save the fabric of society or join the labour force and plug the skill gap in the economy has been a source of considerable doctrinal confusion.

In a speech reported in July 1990, the former Prime Minister, Margaret Thatcher, characteristically sought to strike a balance between the needs of the economy and support for traditional family values. She questioned whether state intervention was either necessary or appropriate, and went on:

It was for business to attract women back to work by offering child care facilities, flexible working conditions, career breaks and home working opportunities.

Mrs Thatcher nevertheless admitted that:

. . . no matter how hard any woman planned to combine work and family, it was impossible to do everything oneself.
(*The Guardian*, 19.7.90)

And went on to propose the following solution:

You have to seek reliable help – a relative, or what my mother would have called a treasure.

This seems a suitable point to summarize the story so far. The overwhelming impression gained from reading the existing literature is that most – not all, but most – of the problems of women as workers are really the problems of mothers as workers. Women without children may, however, get drawn into the net, particularly if they take certain types of jobs.

Employment practice in the UK is not at all sympathetic to the needs of mothers. It is sometimes argued that this is a necessary price to be paid for a lean and fit economy but international comparisons are instructive here, since other countries have found the necessary price not to be quite so necessary after all.

Maternity leave is the most basic form of entitlement for working women. The UK is the only country in the European Community in which statutory maternity leave is not available to all employed pregnant women. The only maternity entitlement available to all is paid time off for antenatal care. All other entitlements have qualifying conditions relating to hours and length of service and in a recent study, 40% of women were found not to qualify for the right to return to work after having a baby. The figure was even higher for semi- and unskilled manual workers.

For those women who are eligible, the state scheme in the UK entitles women to 40 weeks leave; this is paid at 90% of earnings for the first six weeks, followed by a low, flat rate payment for 12 weeks and no payment at all for the remaining 22 weeks.

These UK figures may be compared for illustration with those of Germany, where virtually all women receive 14 weeks leave on full pay, or Italy, where they receive five months leave on 80% of their previous earnings.

As has already been pointed out, women who choose not to return to work immediately after having children often face direct and indirect discrimination when they do rejoin the labour force. Properly organized career breaks, offered and taken up with the full support of the woman's employer, are very rare in this country and getting rarer as the recession bites deeper. They also tend to be restricted to women in managerial and professional occupations.

A number of studies have been carried out into when and why women decide to return to paid work after having children (e.g. Brannen and Moss, 1988). At the most basic level – should a mother of young children take on paid work at all? – attitudes have changed dramatically since the last war, with both women and employers becoming much less traditional in their attitudes to women's gender roles.

As fewer and fewer people held strictly to the notion that 'a woman's place is in the home', employers seized their opportunity and modified the kind of jobs on offer to accommodate to – or capitalize on – women's changing availability and attitudes towards paid work.

Attitudes towards hours of work are more complicated and it is not always clear what is cause and what is effect. In the study of attitudes previously cited, Dex concluded:

> The shortage of suitable jobs appeared to play a large part in the involuntary nature of women's hours of work but other constraints like child care, and husband's hours of work or financial problems also contributed ... It is clear that a woman's decision to work fewer hours is heavily constrained most notably by the presence of children and child-care problems which this raises. These constraints far outweigh the direct effect of traditional attitudes.

What mattered, in other words, was women's 'acceptance of being primarily responsible for child care', which had 'a very definite indirect effect on her behaviour'.

Such processes act to limit mothers' hours of work. The main process acting to increase them is 'wanting or feeling the need of the extra cash'. The hours that a particular mother actually works are therefore invariably a compromise between her personal preferences, her financial circumstances, her other obligations and the constraints imposed by the job market at that time and place.

When accusations are made that employers and governments exploit the female workforce, particularly the part-timers, the defence is usually made that this is the pattern of work that women want. Support for such assertions comes from the ongoing surveys of 'British Social Attitudes', in which the great majority of respondents prefer 'traditional' arrangements for the families of preschool children, i.e. father working fulltime and mother not working outside the home at all. Even when children are in their teens, the preferred arrangement is one in which the mother works part-time rather than fulltime. Women are no more likely than men to approve of mothers of young children going out to work and different social class and income groups also share similar views.

The figures are compelling and must be taken seriously. Quite what they tell us is harder to decide, since with women's employment rates rising steadily, attitudes and behaviour clearly do not coincide. Two additional findings of the BSA surveys may be relevant: the younger the respondents, the less traditional the attitudes; and unmarried people, even allowing for age, seem to be less traditional than married ones.

It is dangerous to speculate about what people 'really want'. However, to counteract the tendency to take stated preferences entirely at face value, it is worth spending a little more time considering the enormous practical constraints upon women's employment decisions.

As has been demonstrated many times over, people generalize from what they know. A woman whose domestic obligations are very burdensome may decide it would be unfair on her children and spouse to divert time and energy to paid work; it is then a short step to the more general belief that, given the problems that would be caused, women like herself should not engage in paid work.

DOMESTIC ROLES

The main findings from research in this area can be summarized very briefly indeed. In most homes, much the greater part of domestic work is done by women, irrespective of their employment status and whether or not they have children. Households in which domestic work is shared equally are very much in the minority, a pattern which has changed little over the time period in which women's employment rates have changed very much (Brannen and Moss, 1990).

One British study of the 'transition to parenthood' (Moss *et al.*, 1987) revealed that the arrival of a couple's first child led to traditional role behaviour becoming even more pronounced:

> Domestically, the division of childcare replicates the pattern already established in housework, which itself seems little disturbed by the addition of children. Having a child therefore seems to accentuate, but not fundamentally alter, a process going back to the beginning of marriage – when the division of housework begins to evolve and when many women subordinate their employment needs to those of their husbands.

Importantly, although the general division of work seemed to be expected by respondents in this study, there was no evidence that they preferred it:

> Parents' "ideal" work–home arrangements and indicators of maternal dissatisfaction with their position suggest that the division of workload evolving after birth was not generally preferred.

Any efforts which women might make on a personal level to increase the amount of domestic work done by men have the odds heavily stacked against them. To begin with the obvious, most household work is unrewarding and some of it is positively unpleasant. Men therefore have to be very motivated to go against the social norms which obligingly excuse them from such activities.

In similar vein, men may feel ambivalence about their wives working, not only because of a fear that this reflects badly on their ability to support their families but also because a working wife is more likely to press for help with child care and housework. The more she contributes to being a 'breadwinner', the more valid becomes the claim that he should reciprocate and contribute to domestic work (Rapoport *et al.*, 1978).

Less obviously, but just as inexorably, pressures deriving from men's work also act in the direction of maintaining traditional arrangements. As Charles Handy pointed out in a paper revealingly entitled 'Going against the grain: working couples and greedy occupations' (1978):

Managers are expected to be highly committed to their jobs and to the organization, particularly if they want to advance ... Social norms, rightly or wrongly, still push the male into the main work-role, and the women into the back-up caring functions for husband and children ... Couples who accept and conform to these norms and expectations go "with the grain" of social forces in their occupational environment. Couples who go against the social grain in attempting to fashion full working lives for both partners when one is in a "greedy occupation" have a different, probably greater, set of strains and conflicts to deal with.

Couples in which one partner wants to go with the grain and one against it presumably have more conflicts and strains still.

CARE ARRANGEMENTS FOR PRESCHOOL CHILDREN OF WORKING MOTHERS

As has been shown, even in the absence of children, women's greater share of domestic work ensures that their employment choices are more constrained than are those of men. Once children have to be taken into consideration, the practical limitations on choices become inescapable.

A great deal has been written about the provision of child care, the social, economic and political factors that determine it and the effects it may or may not have on the development of children. Nearly all of this work is about the care of preschool children; so although the problems of reconciling such care with the demands of paid work are far from being solved, they are at least widely recognized and discussed.

Once again, the main facts are clear. Provision of child care in the UK comes nowhere near meeting a high and growing level of demand and indeed is substantially poorer than in most other European countries. Variation in the provision of publicly funded child care places has been exhaustively documented in reports prepared for the European Commission's Childcare Network. Recently these have been usefully summarized in a publication from the Institute of Public Policy Research (Cohen and Fraser, 1991):

> Overall, the levels of services for children under three are low, although Belgium and France have places for 20% of this age group and Denmark has 48% either in publicly run day nurseries or with employed childminders. This compares with 2% of UK children under three within local authority day nurseries; many of these places are only available to children in need.

And for slightly older children:

> In Belgium and France, nursery education is available, predominantly on a fulltime basis, to over 95% of three and four-year-olds. In France, nursery schools are open eight hours a day . . . In contrast, in the UK, only a quarter of three and four-year-olds are in nursery education, and this is largely part-time.

Since there are far more mothers working than publicly funded child care places, it is necessary to know where the rest of the children are. The most recent figures on care arrangements for the under-five age group as a whole reveal the following (OPCS Monitor, 1992): 21% of mothers used nursery schools, 20% relied on unpaid family or friends, 14% used private or voluntary facilities, 9% a paid childminder or nanny, 6% a local authority scheme and 1% a workplace nursery. In total, 70% of parents made some sort of child care arrangements for their under-fives.

Discussion of preschool child care can be very easily sidetracked – by accident, but often also by design – into moral debates about whether mothers should or should not take on paid work, the 'should' referring to purported harmful developmental consequences for their children.

An up to date review of research and practice in five countries (Melhuish and Moss, 1991) shows, however, that day care is so diverse in nature and quality that any attempt to prove 'it' does or does not have damaging consequences for children is misguided, or intentionally misleading, or both. Further, since social policy considerations shape the kind of child care which different countries provide, and since adequate care is the exception rather than the rule, it seems at least disingenuous to treat the child development outcomes of this care as unqualified scientific facts. Better quality care, it seems plausible to argue, might lead to better consequences for children.

THE CARE OF SCHOOL AGE CHILDREN

By contrast to the mass of material written about the care of preschool children, virtually no attention has been paid to the difficulties women have in meeting their family and employment obligations once their children have entered school. Even defenders of traditional family values concede that paid work and child rearing can be compatible at this stage in family life and judging by the large jump in mothers' employment rates once children enter school, a great many women seem to agree with them.

Of the limited information available, most concerns the care arrangements made for children during school holidays and during those hours when school is over but the ordinary working day is not. The recent OPCS survey provides a useful snapshot: among mothers of children with a youngest child between five and nine, 23% used unpaid family or friends during school holidays and 18% used them for out-of-hours care; 7% used a paid nanny or childminder for holiday care and the same number for out-of-hours care; 2% used a private or voluntary scheme for holiday and again for out-of-hours care; 2% used a local authority scheme (1% out-of-hours); and 1% used a workplace nursery (0% out-of-hours).

The above information was obtained by asking women about the arrangements that they made. Few other sources of data are available, reflecting the now familiar fact that the care of children is regarded as a private matter, with state contributions to care only being justified for especially vulnerable groups.

One form of care rather more visible than the others is the playscheme. This is a service provided by local authorities, or voluntary or charitable organizations, to look after children and provide them with play activities out of school hours and in the holidays. A survey by Petrie and Logan (1986) of local authority involvement in playschemes found that most departments spent little or nothing on such schemes, but one department spent well over a million pounds a year. Those departments which were involved in playschemes were more likely to be supporters of voluntary schemes than providers of places themselves.

Apart from one-off surveys carried out for research purposes, no satisfactory information is available on playschemes nationally, e.g. with regard to numbers of children catered for, whether they are open access or only for 'at risk' or handicapped groups, staff levels and training, space and facilities and so on.

Kids Club Network, a charity that campaigns for out-of-hours care, estimated that in 1991, places were available for less than 1% of school age children. The mismatch between these figures and women's employment rates is enormous and demonstrates vividly that UK child care policy for this age group consists principally of turning a blind eye.

Since in practice it is women who continue to take responsibility for child care, when a mother of a school age child wishes to do paid work, she has to arrive at a new compromise between financial and other factors which might encourage her to work and the care arrangements necessary for that work to be possible.

A common solution is, of course, to work part-time. However, by opting for this course of action, women effectively opt out of successful employment tracks, since part-time workers are not usually treated as serious candidates for promotion and other kinds of career progression. Opting for fulltime work means coping with the child care problem. The option that many women would prefer, at least for a few years, would be to work hours that coordinated with school hours but in jobs and with prospects that fitted their qualifications and experience. For most women, unfortunately, this option is not available and 'downward occupational mobility' is the result.

CARING FOR THE ILL CHILD

From the working parent's point of view, after-school and holiday care at least have the virtue that they can be planned in advance. Childhood illness creates quite a different set of problems. While for most families, illness episodes are inevitable, their occurrence is almost totally unpredictable.

Just how common is childhood illness? Episodes severe or troubling enough to warrant a visit to the GP are relatively well documented. Figures from the Third National Morbidity Study show that for every 1000 children aged 5–14 on a general practitioner's list, there were more than 2000 reported consultations a year (Royal College of General Practitioners, 1986). Two thirds of children had consulted their doctor at least once in the previous year: 21% had consulted once only, 14% twice, 9% three times and 20% more than three times.

It must also be remembered that, since families often contain more than one child, the number of consultations from the mother's point of view may be two or three times the figures given above.

These figures on consultation rates are themselves revealing, but only tell a very small part of the story. Up to 90% of minor illness episodes are known to be diagnosed and treated at home (Spencer, 1984). Most child health care is undoubtedly carried out without the involvement of professionals; most of it is carried out, by mothers, at home. Hannay (1979) acknowledged this when he said that GPs witness only the tip of the illness 'iceberg'.

More detailed information on childhood illness episodes is hard to find, even for those episodes in which professional care is involved. Again, information from a one-off research study helps to fill in some of the gaps.

This was a project carried out in more than 60 general practices in the north of England, caring for about 75 000 children. About 28% of children in the 5–11 year age band were found to have suffered from a cough – one of the commonest childhood complaints – in the previous month and about a quarter of them had consulted a GP about it (North of England Study, 1990).

All of this raises the question as to why some illness episodes are managed at home and others are not. It is not simply a matter of illness severity. Consultation rates are certainly much higher for severe episodes than for milder ones but at almost any given level of severity of, say, a cough, then some children will be taken to see their GP and others will not. The 'decision to consult' is not taken lightly by parents and a number of studies have shown the complex weighing up of different factors, medical and non-medical, which precedes the decision (Wyke and Hewison, 1991).

A number of social and demographic variables, such as mother's educational level, and various proxies for social class (car ownership, owner occupancy) have been found to be related to the decision to consult (Campion and Gabriel, 1984; Wyke *et al.*, 1990). Basically, families in poorer circumstances have higher consultation rates; this seems to be a direct reflection of their children's poorer health, rather than any tendency to 'over-use' the health service (Wyke *et al.*, 1991).

Very little else is known about the factors that influence the decision to consult or, more generally, the way in which families provide health care for their children. In one of the studies mentioned above (Wyke *et al.*, 1990), an initial association was found between mother's employment and consulting the doctor, with women who did not have a paid job being considerably more likely to consult. This relationship disappeared when characteristics of the cough episode itself were taken into account, suggesting that in this sample at least, the mothers 'at home' were caring for children with more troublesome health problems.

In another study, using similar measures but on a very different sample, a contradictory finding was obtained (Clarke and Hewison, 1991). Here, mothers who were employed, and particularly those who had manual jobs, were more likely to be consulters.

The first of these two studies was carried out in the north of England. The sample was drawn from urban and rural areas but consisted almost entirely of white families indigenous to the area. The sample also contained quite a high proportion of families caring for a child with a relatively serious health problem. The second study, by contrast, took place in practices in inner city Leeds, serving an ethnically and culturally very mixed population. Children with severer problems were not deliberately selected for this study, so the average severity level of episodes was lower.

It is not possible to be certain, but it seems likely that these different sample characteristics have led to the apparently contradictory results. The employment opportunities for women in the two samples were very different and it also seems plausible that mothers of children with chronic or recurrent health problems – of which there were more in the first study – are less likely to take on paid work, precisely because of the child care problems that are entailed.

Neither of these two projects was designed to look in detail at mothers' employment and the consequences it might have for child health care. We decided that such a project was long overdue. The available employment and health data did not seem to fit: many children of working mothers were having episodes of ill health without it being at all clear who was available to care for them. It could not of course be assumed that all illness episodes requiring a GP consultation also required absence from school and hence disruption to parents' work arrangements; but it was at least plausible to assume that many of them did so. The consultation itself might require time off work. And it also seemed likely that some kinds of episodes would require school absence but not a visit to the GP – a mild episode of diarrhoea and vomiting, for example.

How were these conflicts of interests managed? Did children of working mothers have less school absence than their peers? Did the mothers stay home from work and provide the health care themselves? Did they arrange for somebody else to provide it? And was all this fairly straightforward for most mothers, or was it a real problem? What were the effects on the mothers themselves?

To throw some light on the last question, one more area of existing knowledge was investigated, namely the effect of employment on women's own psychological health.

WOMEN'S EMPLOYMENT AND
PSYCHOLOGICAL WELL-BEING

In a classic study of psychological health and illness, Brown
and Harris (1978) found that having a paid job reduced the
risk of depression in working class women with young
children. Authorities have argued since then that having a job
improves a woman's self-esteem and it is this that protects
her against depression. Others have emphasized that social
involvement and social support are higher in women who work
outside the home and that these confer emotional benefits.
Others again have suggested that occupying several different
social roles is better for mental health than occupying only one
or two ('wife and mother').

These findings might at first sight seem counter-intuitive:
if paid work brings benefits, it does at least seem plausible
that juggling work and family carries costs. Some research
does seem to support this position. Voydanoff and Donnelly
(1989), for example, found an increased risk of depression in
mothers of young children, whether they were employed or
not. This was in contrast to the picture for married women
without children, where employment decreased their risk of
depression.

The more research that has been carried out on this topic,
the more complex and even contradictory the results have
seemed to be. Bartley and colleagues (1992), for example, found
that having a paid job bore a stronger relationship to psychological health in working class than in middle class women.
Further, the psychologically 'healthiest' women in this study
were those who worked part-time in professional or managerial
occupations; the psychological health of comparable women
who worked fulltime was in fact slightly worse than those with
no paid work.

In this study, psychological health was also related to
domestic conditions: women with heavier burdens of domestic
responsibilities (more children in the household, presence of
person over 75 in the household, lone parenthood, etc.) were
at much greater risk of psychological symptoms than women
with lighter loads.

Synthesizing their own and other recent studies, Bartley
and colleagues conclude that:

Women with full and part-time paid work are more likely to experience lower levels of physical and psychological symptoms than housewives. Part-time work appears to be more advantageous than fulltime, and the benefit is greater in terms of psychological than physical well-being.

Speculating on the explanation of their findings, the authors favour the 'role enhancement' that paid employment brings, but also note that:

Although paid work must represent an additional workload for women, it also makes a considerable difference to house-hold income and removes some women from the poor material circumstances of the home. These factors may balance out the potential negative effects of combining a high domestic workload with paid employment.

The complex nature of the relationship between employment, domestic responsibilities and psychological well-being was also illustrated in an American study (Ross and Mirowsky, 1988), which found:

Employed mothers who have no difficulty arranging child care and whose husbands share child care have very low depression levels, comparable to employed women without children, and to husbands. For non-employed wives, children increase depression levels. Employed mothers who have difficulty in arranging child care and have sole responsibility for child care have extremely high depression levels. Children and their care have no effect on husbands.

Child care arrangements, specifically non-homebased child care arrangements, were also found to be significant predictors of psychological stress in a UK study of dual-earner families by Lewis and Cooper (1987). It would seem therefore that in some circumstances problems with child care can completely overshadow the psychological benefits that are usually associated with paid work.

In a follow-up study, Lewis and Cooper found that employer attitudes could also contribute to stress levels in working mothers. A manager, for example, might warn a woman against 'taking advantage' if child care responsibilities had made her five minutes late for work, or generally 'make her life a misery' to encourage her to leave and take her work–family problems with her.

WHO BEARS THE COSTS OF CARING FOR CHILDREN AND THEIR HEALTH?

It is only in the most superficial sense that the low level of public expenditure on child care services in the UK can be defended as a prudent saving of public funds. A strong contrary case can be made:

> This has not been a low cost option, but an allocation of the costs to others ... Furthermore, there are heavy long term costs involved in failing to commit public funds to child care. These costs are borne by women, by children, by child care workers and by employers. There are also ... significant costs for government, in terms of tax revenue foregone and expenditure on social security benefits.
>
> (Cohen and Fraser, 1991)

Dex writes:

> Women have gone out to work despite the lack of availability of adequate child care provision, despite the absence of late night shopping, and despite the lack of husbands' participation in domestic work.

She goes on:

> Given that women's jobs, and especially when they are part-time in Britain, are low skilled and have poor conditions, it is not unreasonable to argue that work may well not be intrinsically attractive for many women.

Women do paid work because, like men, they need to and they want to; and drawing the dividing line between need and want is difficult except for those who are financially the hardest pressed. A woman might want a higher standard of living for her family; she might want her children to have the things that other children have. To achieve these goals, most women are obliged to accept conditions of work that few men would tolerate, while being relieved of none of their domestic responsibilities.

Yet, we are told by defenders of the status quo that our current practices represent the pattern of work and domestic life that women want and have chosen. This assertion wilfully ignores the socially imposed constraints on women's choices. A rather more realistic claim might be that only after the needs, wishes and preferences of children, partners and employers have been respected does it become a woman's turn to choose from those options that remain.

Concluding with the specifics of child health care, comparisons with other countries are very revealing. In some member states of the EEC, family leave is available to allow mothers or fathers to care for sick children or other family members. Paid leave is available in Germany and Denmark. Portugal, Spain and Italy allow unpaid leave. Some limited provision is made in Greece. In the remaining six member states inlcuding the UK, there is no explicit right to time off work to care for sick children. In the 1980s, a CEC draft Directive on Parental Leave and Leave for Family Reasons, which would have set minimum standards for these types of leave within the EEC, was not adopted, mainly due to the opposition of the UK government.

To rub salt into the wound, in Sweden provision is generous beyond UK mothers' wildest dreams: 90 days family leave per year (CEC, 1990). The policy is explicit: child care, including child health care, is regarded in Sweden not just as a matter of public expenditure but as a sound investment, contributing to an efficient labour market and a prosperous economy.

Back in the UK, whenever their children become ill, many mothers have to perform a complex juggling act, perhaps at very short notice and in a hurry, in order to reconcile their family and employment obligations. On the basis of everything known about child care and 'working mothers', it seems highly likely that the costs – financial and otherwise – of providing this care are borne almost solely by the mothers.

We wanted to know if this was true and we also wanted to know how they did it. The making of social policy usually reflects, directly or indirectly, a totting up of costs and benefits; as long as some costs remain unspecified, then they will be omitted from the totting up exercise, to the advantage of some and the continuing disadvantage of others. We wanted to provide new information about the costs, broadly defined, of caring for the health of children and that is how the 'Parents' employment and child health care' project came about.

2

The research project in Leeds

This chapter describes how the questions raised in the Introduction were turned into a specific research project.

To recap, we wanted to compare how episodes of illness in school age children were managed in families where the mother was engaged in paid work and in families where the mother was 'at home'.

We wanted to collect this information from ordinary families, not the high profile 'dual-career' families much investigated by researchers in the past. To get a good mixture of the kind of people we wanted to talk to, it was decided to recruit families via the schools attended by their children and to choose schools in ordinary areas of a typical UK city or large town. Adjectives can cause problems here; 'ordinary' can carry negative connotations unintended by us, 'typical' invites the retort that every town and city is unique. By 'ordinary', we mean that the areas were not particularly prosperous, but not particularly deprived either; and we mean also that most of the residents would have left school at the earliest opportunity, as is common practice in Britain as a whole. By 'typical' we mean that many other towns and cities would have a similar mixture of inhabitants and would offer a similar mixture of economic opportunities.

The study was carried out in Leeds, in stable, 'working class' areas of the city with few families from ethnic minority groups. Areas like the ones chosen can be found in almost every large city in the UK. That said, it must of course be acknowledged that confining the study to families living in such areas will inevitably have influenced the extent to which the study findings can be generalized. The sample contained, almost by definition, relatively few upwardly and geographically mobile families; and such families may solve their child care problems in quite different ways. Increased access to financial resources may enable them to pay more for child care, for example, but an absence of relatives living locally may limit the opportunities for more informal care arrangements.

Is it possible to generalize from Leeds at all? The employment experiences of women in Leeds may not reflect the national picture, as 'Labour markets are significantly structured by both sexual segregation and by locality' (Walby and Bagguley, 1990). In other words, women's employment histories are likely to differ across different sectors of industry and in different regions within the UK. Further, the responses of employers to the child care needs of their employees are also determined by prevailing local labour market conditions, leading, for example to the present position in which the majority of workplace nurseries are located in the south.

We acknowledge these factors and make no claim that our findings would exactly reflect women's experiences in Belfast, Cardiff or Dundee. We strongly believe, however, that the main messages emerging from our study will 'ring true' in all of those places and many others besides.

To enable readers to make comparisons for themselves, a brief description is required of today's Leeds as a place to live and work. An up-to-date account is particularly important, as Leeds tends to be thought of by outsiders as an industrial city, perhaps with a heyday in the Victorian era. The city certainly did flourish in Victorian times and a good deal of its architecture bears testimony to that but it has changed its character immensely in the last decade or so and now has a successful service economy, particularly strong in banking, finance and the legal sector. According to figures from the Leeds Training and Enterprise Council and the Leeds Development Agency, about 70% of employees in the city work in the service sector, compared to less than 25% in manufacturing. Over 12% of the Leeds workforce is employed in the banking and finance sector and some claim that the city is now second only to London as a financial and business services centre. Service industries in Leeds are predicted to continue their expansion during the 1990s.

Leeds has a population of over 700 000 and a workforce of around 360 000 people. It is a regional centre for retailing, for health care and for education and training. It has always had a relatively high female employment rate compared to similar cities, because many women worked in clothing and textiles even in the heyday of manufacturing industry. Today, the service sector provides overwhelmingly the greatest number of jobs for women in the city.

Compared to, say, Liverpool or Sheffield, with their less prosperous local economies, Leeds offers more opportunities and more choices of employment for both men and women workers, even in a time of recession. That said, we would argue that if the problems of working mothers in Liverpool are worse than those in Leeds, this will be in degree rather than in kind. Similarly, our study was carried out before the present recession began to bite. The recession will have the effect of reducing employment opportunities and generally making life more difficult for those with work and without it; the decision to seek or to take work may be made differently in these circumstances. We accept that, but again would argue for a shift down a continuum of difficulty, rather than a qualitative change of state.

Having satisfied ourselves that studying families in Leeds was an appropriate as well as a practicable means of meeting our objectives, other decisions needed to be made.

Beginning with the age range of the target children, it would have been unmanageable to look at the care of children right across the school years of five to 16, so an early decision was taken to concentrate on children six to seven years old. At this age, children still require a great deal of looking after; they also get more minor illnesses than older children. They are, however, well settled into the routine of school and their mothers have had a chance to adapt to the new circumstances that school entry brings.

We also decided at an early stage to exclude from the study families in which there was a preschool sibling of the target 6–7-year-old child. This was done on the grounds that the employment decisions faced by mothers in such families are likely to be very different from those faced in families where all the children are in school. All other families having a child aged six to seven registered with one of the study schools were eligible to participate.

After some initial calculations about the numbers of children in a school class and the proportion of those likely to have preschool brothers and sisters, we identified five suitable schools. All were located in traditional, predominantly white, 'working class' areas of the city and its satellite areas. Most families lived in Victorian terraced housing or on housing estates that belonged, or had once belonged, to Leeds City Council. Initial approaches were made to headteachers and governing bodies and we were very pleased when all five schools agreed to take part in the project.

Having identified suitable locations for the study, the next task was to develop our methods for gathering the information we needed from families.

The purpose of the project was to monitor children's illness episodes and their effects on a child's family as the episodes occurred over a period of several months. That is to say, we wanted to ask questions about each specific episode, soon after it had arisen. A simpler method of collecting information would have been to ask families general questions about child care and the management of illness episodes, say, over the previous six months. We rejected this second approach, because we wanted to relate child care and employment decisions to the particular characteristics of each episode – what kind of illness it was, how severe, how sudden its onset and so on. Apart from the problems inherent in asking people about events which might have occurred six months ago, we did not want information on what people thought they usually did, but rather on what they had actually done this week or last.

We wanted to conduct three types of interview with each family. The Phase I interview would collect basic descriptive information on families' social and demographic characteristics and detailed information, as applicable, on the mother's work, her reasons for working and the arrangements made for help with child care. Phase II interviews would monitor the management of particular episodes of childhood illness and would be symptom specific (respiratory episodes, gastrointestinal episodes and so on). Depending on the number of illness episodes experienced by the target child, families might be interviewed several times during this phase, once, or not at all. Phase III interviews would address the mother's satisfaction with various aspects of child health care and the family arrangements needed to provide it and look also at the stresses imposed on the family by such provision.

In the paragraph above, we refer to seeking information from mothers. Strictly speaking, we wanted to seek information from the principal carer of the study's target child. We anticipated that in the overwhelming majority of cases, this would be the child's mother and so it turned out to be. That said, the study did identify one lone father.

THE PROJECT TIMETABLE

The project proper began in January 1989. In the months until Easter, visits were made to schools to meet teaching staff and to collect information about the numbers of eligible children on roll, i.e., children who would be 6–7 years old in the autumn of that year and with no preschool child in the family. In one school, similar families with children in the next highest school class were also identified as potential participants in a pilot study.

During the rest of the school spring term, the Phase I interview was designed and piloted. Topics covered were: detailed questions, as appropriate, on the mother's own job and that of her partner; on why the mother was working, both generally and why this particular job and these particular hours; on the mother's perception of her employer's attitude to family commitments; and on the arrangements she made for child care during school holidays, after school hours and during a recent episode of childhood illness.

The interview consisted mainly of questions with precoded replies, with question stems and precodes drawing heavily on previous relevant work, e.g. on women's employment, travel arrangements, etc. For example:

How do you travel to work?

had precodes:

walks/own car/bus/train/other (specify) . . .

On topics where we had less information on which to base precode categories, the questionnaire allowed for women's responses to be taken down in full, for subsequent postcoding or qualitative use as appropriate. For example:

Why did you decide that (child) could go into school?

....

In the school summer term of 1989, a revised list of eligible families was drawn up. The schools collectively provided the names of 159 children. Of these, 12 proved not in fact to be eligible, usually because there was a baby at home of which the schools were unaware or the child left the school after the first interview. One hundred and forty seven families were therefore asked to take part in Phase II of the study; eight declined, so the final sample consisted of 139 families living in and around Leeds.

During the same period that the Phase I interviews were being conducted, the Phase II interviews needed to monitor the management of illness episodes were being developed and piloted. These were symptom specific and whenever possible drew heavily on similar questionnaires developed in previous research. Again, in the interests of efficient data processing, questions with precoded replies were used whenever feasible: for example:

Did (child) have both vomiting and diarrhoea, or just one of those?

had precodes:

Yes, both/No, just vomiting/No, just diarrhoea/Other

The main monitoring phase of the study ran for 7–8 months in the autumn term of 1989 and the spring term of 1990. This period of the year had been deliberately chosen for the study, as child health problems are at their most frequent in the winter months. During this period, Phase II interviews were conducted with study families as illness episodes arose.

The main means we had of identifying that an illness episode had taken place was absence data from the child's school. With parents' approval, school registers were checked every two weeks to see if any of our target children had been absent during that period. The mothers of these children were then contacted and an interview conducted soon after – ideally within the following week. Teachers also told us about any children who had been sent home from school due to illness and their parents were also contacted.

Originally, we had planned a third means of identifying illness episodes, namely asking teachers if any of the target children had attended school with a heavy cold or other condition which, in the teacher's judgement, could legitimately have been the cause of an absence from school. Very few episodes were identified in this way and most of them were mentioned by a particular teacher who felt strongly that some parents sent children to school who should not have been there. In other words, we found that this part of the exercise was telling us more about differences between teachers than differences between children or families. For the greater part of the study, therefore, we only interviewed parents of children who had been absent or sent home from school.

In addition to detailed material on the nature and severity of the illness episode itself, the Phase II interview covered: absence or time off work by the mother and other family members; consequences of this absence in terms of lost income or holiday time, or hours to be made up elsewhere; whether the burden or any loss was borne by the mother alone or shared with other members of the family; reports of employer attitudes and reactions; who else was involved in caring for the child and what form this care took; reasons for deciding to keep the child off school and when to send the child back to school; decisions about consulting the GP; medication – prescription, over-the-counter and home remedies; problems of ensuring compliance with medication; the length of the illness episode.

After the interviews were over, a detailed numerical measure of severity of the episode was calculated for the most common condition, namely coughs and colds. This was based on mothers' replies to a number of questions about symptoms, duration and so on and followed a scoring procedure devised in consultation with a community paediatrician (Wyke *et al.*, 1991). The purpose of this exercise was to let us see if different types of families managed similar episodes in similar ways. Put another way, comparisons could be made between the severity of illness episodes identified in families of different kinds: was the severity of an episode leading to school absence greater in some families than others, for example?

Phase III of the study began after Easter 1990 and continued to the end of the school year in July. In this phase, each family was interviewed one last time. We fed back to the families their own illness and absence data collected during the monitoring phase and asked mothers how satisfied they were with what had taken place. Were they satisfied with the care they themselves had provided? Were they satisfied with the contribution made by others inside and outside the family? We asked mothers to estimate, for themselves and, as appropriate, for the child's father, what proportion of work absence for the year could be accounted for by: their own sickness, caring for ill children, other family commitments and 'other' – deliberately left unspecified. We took measures of satisfaction with work, family and other life roles and we administered a standard questionnaire (the GHQ-12) to assess the generalized psychological effects of stress.

Using all the information collected, the study attempted to answer the following questions.

- Do children of working mothers have less school absence than children of non-working mothers?
- If children of working mothers have less absence, is this because they are attending school with colds and so on which would lead to time off for children whose mothers are at home?
- Are there any differences in health service use, e.g. in the number of GP consultations?
- How dependent are working mothers on local kin, especially their own female relatives, for stand-in child health care?
- What share of child health care is taken by the father?
- How important is child health care as a contributor to the absence from work figures of female employees?
- What are the (perceived) reactions of employers to women's child health care responsibilities?
- To what extent is the economic burden of child health care shared amongst family members?
- To what extent do difficulties in providing child health care contribute to increasing stress in working mothers?

Although the above questions have been framed in general terms, we fully understood that generalizing beyond our sample of Leeds families would require caution. The answers to some questions, we knew, would be particularly locality-bound.

On the basis of local knowledge, acquaintanceship and ordinary observation, we knew that in the parts of Leeds chosen for the study, mothers of young children would be quite likely to live within easy travelling distance of their own mothers and other members of their extended family. Also from informal observation, we knew that grandmothers were extensively relied upon for stand-in child care, including health care. If this proved to be the case in the data we collected, our conclusions could obviously not be generalized to geographically more mobile families, for whom local kin might not be available to provide short notice, stand-in child health care.

The detailed results of our study are presented, topic by topic, in the chapters to follow. A very brief pen picture is, however, given below to set the scene, to distinguish our study immediately from the tradition of work on dual-career families and to emphasize the most important points of context.

Of the 139 study families, in 97 cases (70%) the mothers were in paid work, either part-time (48%) or fulltime (22%). The remaining mothers, not engaged in any paid work, are referred to, for the purposes of this report, as being 'at home'. Six fathers were unemployed and one was on a government training scheme.

There were 22 lone parents, of whom six worked part-time and seven fulltime. Another three single mothers lived with relatives; they are treated as lone parents for some purposes. All families in the study were white, except for one child who had an Afro-Caribbean mother and a white father.

In describing our sample further, we cannot avoid the problem – well known to social researchers – that any index of social status based on occupation, such as the Registrar General's classification of social class, provides less valid information about women than it does about men. Precisely because of women's very variable and distinctly non-linear employment histories, a woman's job at a particular point in her life can be a very poor indicator either of her qualifications or of the social and cultural world she inhabits. Many researchers prefer to emphasize educational rather than occupational factors as a means of characterizing the people in their studies and we have followed this approach.

Few of the mothers in our study had any education beyond the minimum. Fifteen of the 139 had stayed on until they were 18 years old and nine had left at 17 (presumably after retaking exams); but the remaining 115 had left school at the earliest opportunity. After leaving school, 68 of the mothers had undergone further training, most of them in clerical work although seven had trained as nurses or teachers, and one had a degree. Seventy one had received no further education or training.

Most of the 97 mothers in paid work thought of that work as 'just a job', rather than as a career of any kind. The great majority of the employed women did manual or routine clerical work (46% and 38% respectively); the rest were in occupations such as teaching and nursing.

Of the 109 fathers for whom the information was available, only 12 had stayed on at school beyond the minimum leaving age. Almost two thirds of the fathers currently had manual jobs; some of the remainder had begun their working lives in manual jobs but had moved on, for example, to running their own small garage business.

Owner occupancy was a feature of the sample: 101 out of the 139 families owned their own home. Thirty six families lived in council accommodation, one rented privately and one mother lived with her own parents. Ninety four of the families owned at least one car (25 owned more than one car) and 124 had telephones.

There were few large families and very little overcrowding: in 95 of the 139 families, four or fewer people lived in the house and in only four cases did seven or more people live together.

One other point about housing arrangements deserves mentioning: most families lived very near to their children's school. Of the 139 families, 121 said that school was ten minutes away or less. Twelve thought that school was about 15 minutes away and only six thought it took up to half an hour. In 100 cases, the child walked to school; 31 went by car and the rest by public transport.

Most of the mothers (102) had always lived in the Leeds area and another 21 had lived there for at least 15 years. Eighty percent of the mothers (111) had members of their extended family living in or around Leeds and in 104 cases, relatives were reported to live 'nearby'. The most frequent first mentioned relative was the maternal grandmother, with 79 members of the sample saying that their own mother lived 'nearby'. Thirteen others said one of their sisters lived nearby and 12 more mentioned other relatives. After prompting about other family members in the vicinity, a total of 88 mothers told us that their own mother lived nearby and 50 mentioned a sister or brother.

'Nearby' as a description was not granted lightly. In 77 cases, the mother's first mentioned relative lived less than ten minutes away; in 99 cases, the relative lived less than half an hour away.

Fathers' relatives also had to be considered. Of the 113 fathers for whom information was available, 81 had relatives nearby. Seventy one fathers had their own parents living nearby and brothers or sisters were mentioned in 52 cases.

Looking at the mothers' work patterns in more detail, of the 67 who worked part-time, eight worked less than ten hours a week, 47 worked between ten and 20 hours and 12 worked more than 20 hours a week. The hours worked by the 30 fulltimers also varied, since, for example, primary school teachers work shorter hours than office workers: nine women worked less than 35 hours and 21 worked between 35 and 45 hours a week.

Because we were interested in the compatibility or otherwise of mothers' working hours and the school hours of their children, we made detailed enquiries about when these hours were worked. The answer was very complicated. Sixty of the 97 women in paid work could be described as normally working daytime hours in the week, i.e. some time between 8.30 am and 6 pm. Three worked nights, 14 worked in the evening and one in the early morning. Four worked weekends and the remainder some combination of these arrangements.

We asked if start and finish times were flexible: two thirds of the women said no. We asked if there was any flexibility in the number of hours worked in any one week: again, two thirds said no.

To anticipate a subject treated in much more detail later, it should be noted that the pattern of employment which the mothers exhibited, although treated as a 'given' for the purposes of this study, was itself partly a result of decisions taken by the mothers in view of their family obligations. Many of the women expressed a preference to increase their participation in the labour force. Seventy three percent of the part-time workers said that they would prefer to work more hours if they did not have to take account of their child care needs. Indeed, for most of these women child care needs determined not only the number of hours they felt able to work but also their choice of job; around two thirds of the working mothers stated reasons of convenience when asked about why they had wanted their current job. Similarly, if a woman relied for child care help on her own mother or female relatives, those arrangements might not have been simply a consequence of that woman's work patterns, they might also in fact have determined which jobs she could take and which she could not.

In this whole area, there are many difficulties in deciding what is cause and what is effect. The point being made is not simply an academic one: discussion about women's work patterns is often framed in terms of what women choose to do and the consequences of those choices. What we would wish to emphasize, and what we believe our research illustrates very graphically, is that causality also flows the other way: for many mothers of young children, the number and scale of constraints upon them effectively determine the 'choices' they will make.

A final point needs to be made on the subject of cause and effect. In the chapters to follow, many comparisons are made between mothers who work full or part-time or who are at home. For the reasons given above, these comparisons must be interpreted with caution, since the groups are likely to differ in all sorts of ways besides the defining one of fulltime/part-time/at home. Our data suggest that these differences are likely to be complex and the result of a number of trends pulling in different directions. To illustrate, there were proportionately more of the higher social status jobs amongst the fulltime workers in our sample than amongst the part-timers and the fulltimers also tended to have higher educational qualifications. There was also a tendency for women who had moved to Leeds to have higher qualifications and higher social status jobs than those who had always resided there. However, the incomers were, as would be expected, much less likely to have families living nearby. This meant that across the sample as a whole, any tendency for women with greater family support to have increased levels of participation in the labour force would be offset by the fact that this same group of women was likely to have the fewest educational qualifications and hence a reduced participation in the labour force.

In a very large study, it would be possible to disentangle some of these influences statistically. In our study, subdividing our group of 30 fulltime workers on the basis of qualifications and then again on the basis of whether they were incomers or not produces categories with too few people in them to perform most statistical analyses.

Our strategy is rather to warn readers that when comparisons are made, say, between fulltime workers and women at home, that they should bear two points in mind. The first point is the one made earlier, that overall these groups will differ in many ways besides whether the mother has paid work or not. The second point is that each group is a 'mixed bag': there are some fulltime workers in the study with good educational qualifications and some with no qualifications at all. The same is true for the mothers at home. The difference between the groups is therefore a difference of proportions.

An early theme of this chapter was the extent to which the findings of our study can be generalized beyond their time and place. Local labour market conditions were referred to as important considerations here. We would now add that in areas where the inter-relationships of important personal variables, such as qualifications and geographical mobility, were very different from the ones described here, then great caution would be required. In areas where the patterns were very similar, much greater confidence would be justified.

3

Working and caring for the well child

The main focus of later chapters will be the intersection of family life, employment and child health care, in particular, the difficulties families face balancing employment and child care commitments in the event of a child becoming ill. To understand these difficulties properly, however, it is necessary to begin not in times of illness but in times of health. As Chapter 1 made plain, very little is known about the out of school care received by young school age children in this country. The government maintains that arranging such care is an entirely private matter; and the gap between the employment and child care statistics is, conveniently, no-one's official business.

This chapter fills in some of the gaps for our sample of families in Leeds by examining the problems associated with performing the 'juggling act' during those times when the child is well or at least considered well enough to attend school. The problem of caring for the ill child is then presented within the context of the provision of more routine care.

In Chapter 1 we made the point that, once a child enters school, child care problems do not end; they simply change. The shortness of the school day and the length of school holidays present child care problems for most working parents. Given these difficulties, mothers of school aged children face several choices. First, they may opt not to take up any paid employment once their youngest child has entered school. A second option for mothers is to attempt to 'side-step' child care difficulties by selecting themselves into jobs which allow them to provide most of their children's care themselves, jobs which are regarded as 'compatible' with family responsibilities.

Last, mothers may opt for a greater work commitment and this almost inevitably involves sharing child care with others. The statistics given in Chapter 1 show that, for UK women as a whole, the first option is the least popular. For a great many mothers with school aged children, some special arrangements for reconciling work and family responsibilities are required, even when children remain well and are attending school.

Turning to our own sample, who chose to remain at home? Did working mothers successfully 'side-step' child care problems by taking 'compatible' part-time jobs? And what of the mothers who opted for fulltime work or part-time work outside school hours; what sort of family arrangements were necessary to allow their work and family demands to be met?

THE CHOICE TO REMAIN AT HOME

Thirty percent of mothers in our sample were without any paid employment at the beginning of the study. Remaining at home was not always a matter of 'choice': the decision whether or not to seek paid employment was by no means simple and was constrained by a variety of factors, for example, mothers' perceptions about child care difficulties, or fear of loss of state benefits, or simply the perceived lack of suitable local employment opportunities. However, a small minority of the mothers did perceive a choice and saw themselves as fulltime homemakers and did not want or need to seek any work outside the home.

Mothers who were not in paid employment were asked about their reasons for remaining at home. Several mothers gave more than one explanation for this and the first two reasons mentioned were recorded. In all, 33% gave an explanation concerned with seeing their role as a homemaker, although several of these mothers had previously mentioned child care problems associated with working. For a limited number of mothers, providing after-school care and maintaining the home were seen as more than sufficient to occupy their time. The following explanations were extracted from mothers' accounts recorded at the first interview.

I haven't got time. I have thought about it but it just wouldn't work.

It is a fulltime job looking after four children.

I want to spend my time with my family and my children.

My husband prefers me to stay at home and I always have done. I do believe I should be here for the children, they have a lot of holidays and fitting a job in would be difficult.

I just like being a mum. That is my job.

I made a vow when I got married that I wasn't going to go out to work.

In all, 69% of mothers at home mentioned child care problems as one of the reasons why they were not working or not seeking work. Several mothers specifically referred to the problems caused by the short school day, long school holidays and the inevitable occurrence of childhood illness episodes. The following accounts include those of mothers who had recently given up work because they had experienced difficulties reconciling home and work demands, and in particular because there had been a breakdown in child care arrangements.

I had been working up to six months ago as a part-time sales assistant. My mum was having [child] . . . it was too much for her to manage . . . so I had no-one to have her. Then I rang my employer when one of the children was ill, they weren't a bit sympathetic and said I would have to get in. They didn't care how. So I didn't go back.

I find with them having holidays it is a bit awkward really . . . they seem to have that many holidays. And if she was poorly or anything, I have no-one to look after her.

Well, I want to wait until the children are a bit older, then I may do [work]. I like to be there when they get in . . . school holidays would be a problem.

I have just finished a job actually but I had no-one to look after my children so I had to give up. I was doing part-time cleaning. My next door [neighbour] looked after mine when she came home from her job and I went to my job, but she has moved jobs now so I have no-one to look after mine.

My mum used to look after them, then she was poorly herself . . . so I thought I would pack in work so that I could bring them from school and things.

The few mothers in the sample dependent on state benefits were aware that any of their earnings would be offset by a reduction in benefits. For some mothers working did not seem to present a realistic route out of this 'poverty trap'. Unless mothers felt that they could command a reasonably high wage, given that they might have to pay for childminding, some felt that it was not worth trying to find work. A few accepted low paid part-time work to supplement their state benefits. (At the time of the study it was possible to earn up to £15 each week without a reduction in income support.)

I'd like a part-time job but I can't because of the children. You'd have to pay for childminding and everything, although that extra £15 you can earn on the social would be pretty useful.

I am a one-parent family. I don't see any point going to work while the children are still young. It would have to be well paid – I get everything paid now. They are still not old enough to be left on their own and there are holidays and that.

I did apply for a job recently . . . but with the pay it wouldn't have benefited me. Weighing everything up I would just have gone to work because I wanted to, I would be no better off moneywise.

Financial constraints or the lack of them had a pull–push effect for mothers in the job market. Those mothers remaining at home by choice were largely free from financial constraints which 'pushed' or encouraged other mothers to seek work. In contrast, for those reliant on benefits, financial constraints had the opposite effect and acted as a 'pull', encouraging these mothers to stay at home. However, for the majority of mothers remaining at home, child care problems rather than financial constraints were given as the main reason for not seeking work. These mothers did not feel that, in their own particular circumstances, it was worth attempting the juggling act.

We will move on later to discuss in some detail the arrangements working mothers within our sample made for the after-school and holiday care of their children. However, at a more general level, child care considerations frequently come into play long before a mother takes up a particular job. Concerns about providing adequate child care could determine the number of hours a mother felt able to work, the time of day she worked, the type of work she felt able to undertake and the distance she was able to travel to work. In the following section we will examine the ways in which mothers in the study attempted to 'side-step' child care problems by seeking particular types of jobs which were perceived as compatible with family demands.

JUGGLING WITH WORK PROSPECTS

As described in Chapter 1, most women returning to work after being at home with young children experience some degree of downward occupational mobility. This was certainly the case in our sample. For many mothers returning to work this downward mobility was partly a matter of choice, albeit a choice constrained by family demands. The reasons mothers gave for going out to work had little to do with the nature of their work and the personal satisfaction employment might offer them, but were more concerned with 'needing the money'. As far as seeking a particular job was concerned, in general mothers returning to work did not seek jobs that were well paid, challenging, intrinsically worthwhile or that used their skills and training but, first and foremost, jobs that seemed to offer 'convenience'.

At first sight it seems that there was something of a mismatch when mothers were asked first about their reasons for seeking work and second about their reasons for seeking a particular job. In the first case the reason was money and in the second convenience. The apparent mismatch is, however, easily explained within the context of family life – financial constraints pushed mothers into employment while child care responsibilities pushed mothers into a particular type of job. In accepting a particular type of employment mothers were attempting to balance the many demands being made upon them. In the following section we look more closely at the way these sometimes conflicting demands were reconciled by mothers.

When asked about their reasons for wanting to go out to work, around two thirds mentioned money as their main reason and a further 24% mentioned money if a second reason was given. While some mothers saw their income as crucial for the family, for a lesser number work allowed them the freedom to buy 'extras'.

> ... pocket money ...

> Being a one-parent family I have to work. If I don't work they don't eat.

> Money ... it is not choice, it is necessity.

Mothers were asked specifically about whether they perceived their own earnings as essential or for extras. More than two thirds thought that their wages paid for essentials, while those remaining said that their earnings paid for extras. However, the ways that some mothers qualified their replies demonstrated to us that one person's extras were another's essentials and vice versa. For some mothers having their own car was perceived as essential while one mother mentioned new shoes for her children as being an extra. Several mothers referred to children's clothes as extras.

While money was the over-riding concern for the majority of the working mothers, around a third mentioned other factors as their main reason for wanting to work. A few mothers mentioned the positive stimulation which work offered them, others talked of the negative feelings associated with remaining at home. The following accounts describe the ways in which work offered mothers an escape from domestic boredom or a means of gaining either personal fulfilment or simply company and conversation.

> The reason I do the work I do is that I want to work for myself. I don't get any satisfaction from sitting at home now the children are at school.

> To get me out of the house. I am not a stay at home person.

> It is nice to get paid. It is nice to keep my mind going.

> Boredom. With not knowing anyone round here it breaks my day up.

Company. It gets you out and meeting people.

I did want to go out for my own self-confidence and feeling I was doing something for myself.

I can't stand being at home, it is boring. Any woman can do housework up till dinner, then you have nothing to do.

While remaining at home was regarded as 'boring' or lacking in fulfilment by some of the working mothers, this view was by no means shared by the entire sample. As we have already shown, several mothers were happy to remain at home and found fulfilment in their role as fulltime homemaker. Amongst the working mothers there were several more who were clear that if they did not need to work for the money they would prefer to remain at home.

WOMEN'S JOBS – A MATTER OF CONVENIENCE

Although the majority of working mothers gave money as their main reason for engaging in paid work, when they were asked about choosing their current job, very few mentioned the fact that the job was well paid. Asked why they had wanted this job in particular, more than half of the sample of working mothers gave reasons connected with the job being 'convenient': the job offered 'convenient hours', or it was within a short distance of home, or it offered school holidays. Convenience for these mothers meant compatibility with home demands. By seeking 'convenient' work, mothers attempted to minimize conficting demands on their time and escape from the 'juggling act'.

Although it was not possible to make a strictly objective comparison between previous and current employment, it was clear that many mothers in the sample suffered demotion when they returned to work after having children. While some mothers took up similar work as returners, the fact that they opted for part-time hours usually led to a reduction in pay, status and promotion prospects. For some mothers practically any job would 'do' provided it 'fitted in' with their home commitments. 'Fitting in' almost inevitably meant part-time hours and frequently involved working evening or night shifts or other unsocial hours. 'Fitting in' might also imply work that seemed to offer low demands or 'pressure' as some mothers felt that they could not manage the competing 'pressures' of home and work. It is also important to remember that since few of the mothers in the sample had any academic qualifications or proper vocational training, the majority did not feel that they were in a position to pick and choose in the job market.

Educationally-wise I can't get a good job. And with the hours I want to work – you take what is available these days.

I was desperate financially, I just had to go. I wanted part-time work. I saw the advertisement on the door [of the shoe shop].

Because I could take her [child] to work with me. I wouldn't want anyone else to have her. If I didn't work there I wouldn't work.

Because you could work at home. When I first started it was at home only.

[mother working as a cleaner] I didn't want to go back to M and S because there are pressures and I have enough pressures at home. Cleaning isn't for me although I just wanted a little job.

I just saw it advertised and I thought it was better to work nights with children and it was easy to get there.

For many mothers, 'convenience' was traded for important benefits and working conditions. A relatively large proportion of the mothers, around a third, did not have any paid holidays. A third of the mothers said that they would receive no pay if they were absent from work because of their own sickness. These poor conditions were partly due to employment legislation – some mothers paid no National Insurance contributions because the number of hours they worked was low. However, several mothers worked for cash on a casual basis and expected no benefits from their employers.

One mother who worked fulltime took no official breaks, was not paid for holidays or for sickness, but was allowed some flexibility in terms of start and finish times and allowed time off (unpaid) if either of her children was ill. This woman described her employer as 'very good'.

Although flexibility was prized, it could not always be obtained: more than two thirds of the working mothers reported no flexibility at all in start and finish times or in the number of hours worked. For around a quarter of the mothers there was some flexibility, but as the above account indicates, this was sometimes achieved at the expense of other benefits.

We discuss flexibility in relation to children's illness in Chapter 7. However, it is worth recording here that more than two thirds of mothers reported that they would receive no pay if they were off work to care for an ill child or for other family reasons. Of those that thought that they would be paid many qualified their statements by saying that they would be paid 'only if they made the time up' or swapped shifts with a colleague.

Shift working was a means of achieving 'convenience' for some mothers. More than a third of the working mothers worked shifts of one type or another (38%). Those on nights, weekend and early morning shifts were all working part-time. The most popular shift was evenings; evening work included stacking shelves or cleaning in local supermarkets, cleaning offices, waitressing in restaurants or machining in clothing factories. Fifteen percent of those in work were engaged in evening work of this type.

For mothers working part-time, hours of work were crucial but whether or not the work was nearby also seemed to be an important consideration. As compared with the fathers in paid work, it was much more likely for the mother to live close to her work. Forty three percent of mothers lived within ten minutes of their work while this was the case for only 23% of the fathers in work. It was also more likely that the mother would walk to work rather than travel there by car or public transport. It was clear that, as well as seeking 'convenient' hours, mothers also sought 'convenient' work locations in order to minimize the impact of work on their home commitments. Distance to work and travelling time were less of a consideration for working fathers. One mother summed up her attitude towards her job succinctly:

It was handy, it was part-time and the pay was OK.

This section has shown the extent to which mothers in our study sought to minimize their child care problems by seeking paid work that was 'convenient' and 'compatible' with their family responsibilities. Put another way, the purpose of these arrangements was to enable the mother to provide most of the child care herself, either because she wanted to or, more commonly, because she had in any case no alternative.

In the following section we look at the arrangement and provision of child care as part of the normal school day routine. As a result of this examination of normal family arrangements we will demonstrate that whether or not a mother was in paid work and whether she worked full or part-time, she still bore the brunt of responsibility for providing or arranging for out-of-school hours and holiday child care. We will also show that despite their efforts to 'side-step' child care problems by providing the bulk of care themselves, most of the working mothers still needed to rely on others at certain times of the day, on certain days of the week or during school holidays to help them provide all necessary care for their children. It seemed to be almost impossible to avoid the juggling act altogether.

OUT-OF-HOURS AND HOLIDAY CHILD CARE

Because only tiny numbers of places are available in organized schemes, it is left almost entirely to mothers to patch together child care for out-of-school hours and school holidays. As we will demonstrate, despite mothers' best efforts, such arrangements for care are often complicated and consequently fragile.

As part of the initial interview with mothers, we asked in some detail about the child's normal daily routine. We asked how the child travelled to and from school and who, if anyone, delivered and collected the child from school each day. For those working mothers whose hours extended beyond the school day, we asked about out-of-hours care and for those mothers working weekend, evening, night and other shifts, we asked about the usual child care arrangements while the mother worked.

THE PROVISION OF ROUTINE CHILD CARE

Not unexpectedly, there were differences between mothers at home and those in paid work in terms of the provision of child care. What was unexpected was that these differences were not large: whether or not mothers worked, they themselves provided the bulk of routine child care.

Mothers at home were generally available to deliver and collect their children to and from school and generally did so. Hence such care was largely stable and predictable. Ninety percent of these mothers accompanied their child to and from school at the beginning and end of the school day. If the mother did not take the child to school, a sibling or other relative did so. It was also likely that the mother would be available every day: in only 7% of cases was a second person involved in delivering the child to school and in 19% of cases collecting and taking the child home from school. For these children it was likely that their mothers would be waiting for them at the school gates every day of the week. Even when someone other than the child's mother was involved in collecting the child from school, this was less a matter of providing the mother with 'help' than a reciprocal arrangement with other mothers arranged on a friendly, informal and ad hoc basis. Mothers at home only relied on such arrangements under extraordinary circumstances. The type of 'sharing' arrangement mothers made is described in the following account:

> I take her child in the morning and she collects mine in the afternoon. We reciprocate the favour ... I don't think either of us feels obliged. It is nice to have someone to help you if you are in a jam but I don't think that either of us feels we have to.

For such mothers, sharing child care was an option rather than a necessity. If for any reason either mother was unable to fulfil her side of the child care 'bargain', there would not be any particular problem for the other mother in terms of conflicting demands on their time.

Similarly, such mothers were generally available to provide child care during school holidays and most of them did indeed provide all necessary care at such times. Although all of the mothers in this group said that they were the main carer during school holidays, in about a quarter of cases a second person was involved.

Mothers at home occasionally made reciprocal arrangements with friends, neighbours and relatives for providing holiday or out-of-hours care. However, even when direct reciprocity was not possible, there were no instances of mothers in this group paying directly in cash for child care.

For mothers at home the arrangement of out-of-hours and holiday child care was relatively simple and stable – they saw themselves as available to provide this care and in virtually all cases they did so. For those children whose mothers were in paid work, the arrangements were frequently less simple and potentially less stable.

ROUTINE CHILD CARE AND THE WORKING MOTHER

Although we have used the term 'routine' to describe the care of the healthy child, for many mothers in paid work there was little 'routine' if that term suggests a predictable, stable and simple organization and provision of care. Child care arrangements were in fact often complicated and unstable and therefore potentially fragile if there were any sudden alterations in circumstances. Arrangements for the delivery and collection of the child to and from school frequently involved the mother and at least one other person. Similarly school holiday care was often shared between the mother and other carers. Carers drafted in to assist with child care were often relatives, friends and neighbours, providing care without any direct financial cost to the mother. Only a minority of mothers made more formal arrangements with paid babysitters and childminders. When we examined these seemingly complicated child care arrangements, it became clear to us that, despite work commitments, in most cases working mothers remained the main providers of care for their children: they only relied on others to provide assistance at certain times in the day, on certain days of the week or during certain weeks of the year when providing child care was not compatible with their work commitments.

In 68% of cases working mothers described themselves as the main person delivering their child to school. However, this arrangement was not always possible every day of the week and in more than a quarter of cases a second person helped and in 4% of cases a third. Collecting the child from school was an even greater problem and although mothers remained the most likely person to be collecting their children from school, in more than a third of cases a second person was involved and in 8% of cases a third person was involved. Thus as far as children of working mothers were concerned, a significant number could expect different people to collect them from school on different days of the week. From the child's point of view such a situation could be somewhat unsettling, even though the person deputed to care for them was usually a trusted relative. From the mothers' point of view, such arrangements could present an organizational nightmare.

If the working mother was unable to deliver and collect her child from school herself, she would frequently arrange for close relatives to do so. Overall, apart from mothers, 50 other individuals were involved in collecting and delivering the 97 children of working mothers to and from school. This large group comprised grandmothers, maternal aunts, other (mainly female) relatives, older siblings and to a lesser extent paid carers.

Similar types of arrangements were made by working mothers for school holiday care, although such care, because more prolonged, was if anything easier for mothers to organize than before and after-school care. Despite this in some cases at least two people were involved in providing care on different days of the week.

The provision of holiday care by working mothers was not always a problem. Holiday care was most easily arranged by those mothers in evening, weekend or night work as those arrangements that existed during school terms could remain in place – school holidays did not pose any extra child care problems. Despite such arrangements already being in place, the fact that the child was at home during the day and not in school could increase the child care burden for mothers; for example, a mother working night shifts explained that during school holidays she was unable to get any sleep during the day. A small proportion of the sample did not need to make special arrangements for school holidays as they were employed in schools themselves and could take school holidays; this was the case for those employed as dinnertime supervisors and teachers. Those employed as cleaners in schools, however, often had their hours increased during school holidays rather than shortened. It is also worth noting that some of those working as dinnertime supervisors were either unpaid during holidays or received only a small retainer. The privilege of 'convenience' for these mothers was not bought cheaply. A few mothers who worked for family firms or who worked from home could organize their working day around their child's needs during school holidays, although this might necessitate working late into the evenings or at weekends.

Arranging or providing holiday care caused appreciable burdens for the majority of working mothers. Many were heavily dependent on the help provided by relatives at such times. Nevertheless mothers continued to be the main providers of care and in 60% of cases working mothers claimed that they themselves were the main person providing care during school holidays. For the remaining 40% the main carers comprised grandparents (17), paid babysitters or childminders (6), fathers (3) and other relatives, friends and neighbours (13). For working mothers it was also likely that more than one person would be responsible for providing care: in more than half of the cases (56%) a second person was involved. The extent of involvement provided by grandparents was surprisingly large. More than a third of working mothers relied on grandparents to provide some help in the form of child care during school holidays. Our sample mainly comprised individuals living in fairly close communities, within a short distance of grandparents and other members of the extended family. Heavy dependence by working mothers on grandparents has also been shown in other studies, however, particularly with regard to the care of the preschool child (for example, Presser, 1989). The reliance on other relatives was also strong, although the involvement of the child's father in the provision of holiday child care was less common: even when he was involved, the father was almost always mentioned as the second carer (14 cases).

To summarize, for both out-of-hours and school holiday care the main differences between mothers in and out of paid work were that for the former, providing care was more complicated and potentially more fragile, because it was likely to involve more individuals and different arrangements for different times of the day and week. The common feature across both groups was that the mother herself was the main provider of care.

Although both working and non-working mothers sometimes relied on others to help provide care, the groups differed in the ways in which mothers paid for that help. For mothers at home there were no instances of anyone paying directly in cash for child care services, either for out-of-hours or holiday care. For working mothers, on the other hand, providing child care could incur financial costs. Seventeen per-cent of working mothers paid for some aspect of the delivery or collection or out-of-hours care of their child. Payment for these aspects of care was likely to be fairly low. School holi-day care was more likely to incur costs and such costs were likely to be greater. Around a quarter of working mothers paid for holiday child care: over half of these mothers paid more than £10 per week, with about 10% paying more than £20 per child per week. Thus for a few mothers the financial costs of child care were high, particularly when set against their own largely poor earnings. From our point of view as researchers, measuring the costs of caring was relatively straightforward provided we confined our attention solely to the direct finan-cial implications for mothers. This simple approach could not be justified, however, as even when financial costs were exacted by carers these were often not the limits of mothers' obligations; and mothers who did not pay carers directly in cash for child care services frequently faced a variety of subtle obligations and pressures.

It was possible to describe the 'child care contract' between carers and mothers and the 'exchange rate' for child care services in terms of five quite distinct but often co-existing methods of 'payment'. We have already mentioned that some mothers paid directly in cash for child care services. Such a method of payment for services was regarded by some mothers as the most satisfactory means of settling such costs. In the following account the mother describes how, by paying directly for child care services, she eased her own conscience and did her friend a 'good turn':

> I gave her £5. She doesn't ask for it but I gave it her. I'd rather not put on people. You feel better. Her husband is unemployed.

Despite paying for care in cash mothers might feel other obligations towards carers. When there was no cash payment such feelings were more likely. A second means of paying for child care also involved financial outlay for mothers but was a means of paying carers who might otherwise be reluctant to accept cash payment. In these cases mothers bought 'gifts' for carers – sweets, cigarettes or flowers. In the third form of contract, mothers could pay for child care without financial cost by a direct exchange of services; working mothers could make reciprocal arrangements for the care of children to enable them to meet their work commitments – such exchanges would be explicit and regular. Other forms of service exchange were less explicit and less regular. If a direct reciprocity was not possible, mothers could offer other services to carers; for example, when grandmothers provided child care, mothers could offer to take them shopping or do decorating in exchange. Finally, even when immediate reciprocity was not exacted, mothers might still face indirect costs which could in the long term prove substantial. If relatives, especially grandparents, provided help without any payment in cash, goods or services, the matter of reciprocity was unlikely to disappear but rather to be postponed. As one mother commented, 'There is no direct obligation, but you feel indebted'. A sense of indebtedness was felt by several mothers; for them, the burden of payment for child care was not discharged. Repayment of services was simply being delayed until such time as the needs of the carers were greater.

To summarize the contents of this chapter, we have illustrated how the working mothers in our study attempted to side-step child care problems in a variety of ways; for example, they selected particular types of employers and particular types of employment in terms of hours, location, flexibility and holidays. As a result of these efforts most of the mothers were able to provide most of their child's care themselves. When arrangements were made with others, they were usually of an informal nature involving close relatives and friends and often based on reciprocity rather than direct payment. We have also shown, however, that, even in these circumstances, for working mothers arranging child care could be a complicated business; many children, for example, could expect to see different people waiting for them at the school gates on different days of the week.

Despite being complicated to organize, out-of-hours and school holiday care at least have the virtue that they can be arranged by mothers in advance. In the rest of the book, we will describe what happens when there is a change in the child's routine as a result of illness episodes. Unlike out-of-hours and holiday care, children's illnesses can rarely be anticipated and planned for. We wanted to know how the complicated arrangements made for the care of the healthy child were adapted at times of family stress, such as during illness episodes, and we wanted to know, too, how the costs of caring were distributed amongst family members.

4

Schools and childhood illness episodes

For mothers of six to seven-year-old children, illness episodes which occur during the week and during the school term invariably lead to decisions concerning school attendance. If a child exhibits any kind of symptoms or reports feelings of illness on a school day then the question arises as to whether or not the child should attend school.

A major focus of our research was whether maternal employment in general, and hours of work in particular, had any effect on decision making about school attendance. This raised a series of related questions: for example, did children of working mothers have fewer episodes of illness which resulted in school absence? Was their absence shorter? Were they sent back to school earlier after an illness? Was overall absence less? Did the constraints associated with working fulltime rather than part-time make any difference to school attendance? Was it the case that mothers who were at home were more likely to keep their children off for minor or 'trivial' illnesses? Or did factors associated with maternal employment make no difference to school attendance?

We also wanted to know how mothers explained and accounted for the decision to keep a child away from school and, equally importantly, the decision to send a child back to school after an illness episode. Were there any differences in the types of explanations offered by mothers in paid employment? Who was involved in the decision making process: was it the mother alone or did other family members, health professionals and school staff participate? If so, what kind of influence did they bring to bear?

Berore addressing the specific factors arising from mothers' employment, it first needs to be pointed out that in making their decisions about attendance, mothers also had to take school factors into account. School policies and practices regarding the management of illness episodes (e.g. asthma attacks) within school, the administration of medicines, swimming, PE, 'playing out' (i.e. spending playtime outside) and non-classroom activities such as carol concerts or school trips all had to be taken into consideration. A child that was considered well enough to sit in a warm classroom, for example, might not be considered well enough to spend a lunchbreak in a cold playground. If the school insisted on the latter, that might mean an extension of the time that child was kept away from school.

Mothers mentioned local authority policies on routine medical examinations and disease notification as being other relevant factors in their decision making. Finally, the physical environment of the school was seen as important. Was the classroom too cold? Too draughty? Too stuffy? All these factors could affect decision making in illness situations and indeed, it was only a short step from there to perceiving schools as causes of ill health in some circumstances.

SCHOOLS AS A SOURCE OF ILLNESS

In nearly half the episodes of illness which led to school absence during the monitoring stage of the research, the cause of illness was unknown to the mothers. In the 59% of episodes where a cause was attributed by mothers, in 43 instances (15% of all episodes) there was a specific mention of the child's school as a source, cause or reason for ill health or feigned illness. Schools were regarded as a particularly dangerous source of contagion. If an illness was going around it was assumed that the child had either picked it up from the school premises, for example, from the toilets, or from other children sent to school by uncaring parents while they were suffering from an infectious illness. If a child feigned illness it was regarded by some mothers as a school avoidance tactic. For some children school work was seen as a source of anxiety, which resulted in 'tummy aches' or 'headaches'. School dinners and milk were mentioned also as causes of illness, while school premises and policies regarding 'playing out' were perceived as a particular danger. The following accounts from mothers describe some of the many sources of illness perceived to be school related.

She is funny with weather. Her coat was damp the day before with playing out in the wet and cold. I have noticed that when she plays out in the rain she starts with these temperature dos. It might seem ridiculous to you, but she is always poorly afterwards. I got a bit cross and upset with them making them play out. They throw them all out in the playground. The first year in school was ridiculous – I said she is coming home with clothes wet through and she is poorly. I think they thought I was being funny.

There is a big puddle in the playground, he got absolutely soaked. He sat in those clothes all day. He said he was cold and he looked grey. The day after he complained of a sore throat and earache.

I think it is that classroom. Out of a class of 29 or 30 she had about 14 or 15 in. It is the hottest classroom. There were a couple of kids in the same as him. Their mothers sent them in because they were working.

Well, I thought it was the bullying. I just thought he didn't want to go. When I got home from work his Grandma said he was full of it. He was quite all right.

[constipation] Well, the only thing that causes it is too much milk to drink. Drinking too much milk at school.

SCHOOL ATTENDANCE

As part of the project, school absence was monitored over two school terms. We recognized that absence from school was not synonymous with illness – many children missed school for reasons other than ill health and in some instances, children with illnesses of certain types or certain degrees of severity still attended school. School absence, in other words, was influenced by a variety of factors besides the occurrence and severity of recognizable illness conditions. However, as far as the working mother was concerned, the perceived severity of a recognized illness episode was central to the decision making process. If a child had only minor symptoms and was deemed to be fit for school, then many of the problems associated with managing illness episodes would be avoided. If a child could attend school, then there was a strong chance that the normal routine of caring for that child could remain intact. If on the other hand the child had to be 'off sick', then a whole host of decisions needed to be made concerning the care of the child during school hours.

Further, the decision concerning attendance was not necessarily the end of the matter; if a mother decided to send a child into school with some illness symptoms, then the child might later be returned home by the school. In this case, the mother might feel her competence as a carer was being questioned by teaching or ancillary staff. Several mothers, when explaining their decision to keep a child at home for a relatively trivial illness, described their fear of the child being sent home from school; stigma would clearly be attached to such an event. Children's illnesses were, in other words, regarded as a means whereby school staff and other parents could rate a mother's performance as a mother. As the following account – by a mother who was not in paid work – demonstrates, other parents could be harsh judges.

> There is a lot goes off down at school – chickenpox, measles. They could do better. The head teacher is a bit slack at letting parents know – they should demand that those kids stay at home, it isn't fair to the other kids. There was one kid with mumps! There are one or two [parents] down there that don't care what happens to the kids ... They [school] are not strong enough about kids going into school when they are poorly – if the mother is working or whatever – not strong enough to turn round and say 'Your child is ill, please take it home'.

If, however, a child with a minor complaint was given the benefit of the doubt and kept away from school, the mother might face criticism for the opposite reason – for 'giving in' to a child with either trivial or feigned symptoms. This was seen by some as folly not only because it caused the child to miss school work unnecessarily, but also because it encouraged 'weak' undesirable attitudes.

From the above it can be seen that in the absence of severe symptoms, the decision to keep the child away from school was frequently a difficult one, with no clear 'right' choice of action. If a mother was in paid work, the decision regarding school attendance during minor illness episodes was made even more complicated by the competing claims of the mother's work commitments.

TO ATTEND OR NOT TO ATTEND?

During the first phase of the research mothers were asked to re-call the last time their child had been ill. It was made clear that 'illness' did not only refer to major infectious illnesses or serious surgical operations but 'just the last time [child] was not well'.

In their accounts, mothers described the decisions they had made concerning school and school attendance. Of the 139 mothers who responded to these questions, 16% had decided to send their child into school despite the illness. The decision in favour of school attendance was mainly taken in view of the non-worrying or non-distressing nature of the child's symptoms or condition. There was no evidence that the decision related in any way to maternal employment; the child of a non-working mother was just as likely to attend school as the child of some-one in paid work. More than half of the mothers reported that the nature and/or severity of their child's condition had not merited school absence. Symptoms had either been 'usual' for the child and therefore non-worrying, or confined to a particular time of day or night, or had just been considered trivial.

Because it has just become a regular thing and he is all right once I have given him the medicine.

He is not really ill with it. He can just shrug it off. It is just night time he is coughing.

Well it was at night. I put her back to bed and sat with her. The next morning she was as right as rain.

One mother said that school attendance had been determined by the advice of her GP. In four cases the duration of the illness had been very short and the child had made a 'quick recovery'.

He was fighting fit. He doesn't stop down for long.

In three cases mothers had decided to send their child into school because of the child's previous sickness record and poor school attendance – the child had already had 'too much' time off.

The negotiation of school attendance could also involve school staff:

Well, had she been ill in herself I wouldn't have let her go. I knew [class teacher] would give me a ring if she was not well enough. She knows she can contact me . . . for me to bring her home.

Of those children that had attended school, nine were receiving medication and four of these were taking their medicines into school to be administered by school staff.

MONITORING ILLNESS EPISODES AS THEY AROSE

The majority of children had not attended school during their reported 'last illness'. Despite our prompts, mothers had tended to recall relatively serious illness episodes when asked retrospective questions about their child's health. To counteract this tendency to bias, in the second stage of the research, mothers were questioned about school absence as it arose, provided the child had been off school for health related reasons.

The decision to keep the child off school was frequently multifaceted. School absence implied decisions concerning child care, work absence and possible penalties associated with work absence, lost school work and the care of siblings. School absence was frequently negotiated with the child, other family members and school staff.

During the monitoring stage of the research, there were 282 episodes of illness which led to school absence and which were followed up by interview. Thirty five percent of mothers reported that over the monitoring period the child had had further illness but had not been absent from school, either because the illness had been minor or had occurred during school holidays or at the weekend.

The majority of the children (86%) were absent from school at least once during the seven month monitoring period. The remaining children had no illness related absence between September and March and their mothers were therefore not interviewed at Phase II. The mean number of illness episodes was 2.4 per child, although this figure belies a considerable range in terms of the number of illness episodes and the length of these episodes. Four children were absent from school on eight separate occasions over the 25 school weeks during which monitoring took place, while 19% of children were absent on just one occasion because of illness.

The main cause of school absence was upper respiratory tract conditions – coughs, colds, earache and sore throats. Coughs and colds alone accounted for 97 absence episodes, that is, for about a third of illness related school absence, while vomiting and diarrhoea led to a further 60 episodes.

In many cases the reason given by mothers for keeping their child away from school was the nature and severity of the child's condition. In about half of the episodes at Phase II (52%) this was mentioned as the first reason for keeping the child away from school and where a second reason was given, it was mentioned in a further 15% of episodes. Mothers frequently asserted that their child was just too poorly to attend school or that their child had symptoms that would make it difficult for them to be in school.

She just wasn't fit to go anywhere. She just couldn't be bothered. She had no energy at all. She just laid down.

She said her throat was hurting and she had a thumping head. She loves school so I know she wouldn't say she was poorly to stay at home. Normally she would cry to go to school – but it wasn't like that. She just said OK when I said she couldn't go. It wasn't fair to send her to school when she was feeling sick in case she was sick in the school.

Further, the home environment was seen as being generally conducive to recovery while that of the school was seen as potentially exacerbating illness. School staff were sometimes accused of being careless with regard to seeing that children wore warm clothing when outdoors or failing to take other precautions to ensure recovery from or prevention of illness.

Well with her not being well on Sunday. She looked tired and I knew that she wouldn't have been wrapped up at lunchtime if I had sent her. If they have PE they have to walk out to the other building – walking out in the cold.

Mainly because of his high temperature. They are sent out in all weathers without their coats on.

In addition, home nursing skills, the love and care a mother could provide and the warmth and comfort of home were seen as factors which would both relieve the child's distress and ensure a more rapid recovery. This might be seen to be particularly important if the mother was in paid work, as if somehow she could 'compensate' her child during interludes of illness. The home environment was described as warm and quiet and was contrasted with school where children would be rushed and forced into activity.

I felt that he needed some love and support. As I work most of the time, I like to think that at times like this I am there.

Well mainly because he couldn't eat. I thought if I kept him at home I could give him soup and soft things. They do tend to rush them at school.

I just felt that he needed a rest. I think they recover quicker when they have a rest. He wouldn't have been quiet at school.

They, at school, wouldn't have thanked me and when you are sick there is no place like home – your mum to look after you.

The main reason was that he was miserable and tired. It is not a good atmosphere at school if you feel out of sorts.

Other reasons for keeping the child off school, as well as those specifically connected with the child's condition, were associated with the school itself or school staff. Mothers sometimes kept their children at home from a sense of guilt, or because they were worried that they would appear 'bad' in the eyes of school staff or other parents, particularly if the illness had highly visible symptoms such as a rash or swelling or if the child sounded 'bad'.

... he looked such a sight. I would have looked a bad mother sending him to school.

She wouldn't have done at school. ... You don't want to be thought of as someone that passes bugs on to all the other kids.

I knew she wasn't well, she was really coughing. The teacher had said 'Stop coughing!', so I thought ...

I thought if people were looking they would think I had sent her to school with chickenpox or something.

Some mothers mentioned that they did not want to 'burden' school staff and this was given as their reason for keeping their child away from school.

He weren't right. I'm not going to force a kid like that to go. It is not fair on the teachers to send them like that and I don't think it was fair on my son. He just wanted to sleep and that was that.

Well, I don't think it fair to the teachers to put up with a kid that is off it.

I don't want her sick at school. There is only one teacher with all them kids.

Some mothers perceived that teachers possessed some sort of superior knowledge about child care, about the best way to deal with illness and about what was good for their child. It was sometimes claimed that teachers had given children explicit instructions to stay off, or mothers perceived that teachers 'did not want them in' with certain conditions; ill children could disturb other children or upset classroom management. In some cases, teachers' comments were distressing to children and parents.

The only reason [she was off] was that she had been told by the teacher to stay off. She had nothing wrong the next day. She was distressed about the fact that the teacher had told her not to come the next day – that she couldn't go for the rest of the week. She wanted to go to school but the teacher had said that.

[hayfever]Well basically the teacher said don't bring her back when I picked her up at dinnertime. I think they would rather mums cope with them than have to cope with them at school.

Well, she was a little bit worried. She says the teacher gets annoyed when they keep coughing. She says 'Give up coughing', she was worried that she would get into trouble for coughing.

Well, I don't think she would have served any good purpose

by going and the teacher said 'Keep her off, when she is coughing like that she disturbs the other children'.

Well, the teacher says they don't want them back all coughing.

Occasionally, parents disagreed with the teacher's opinion on the child's condition or the best means of treating the condition. In the following account, given the mother's knowledge of her child and the family circumstances, the teacher's action seems inappropriate.

Well, it was the school that sent him home. I took him to school as normal – he was fine. Then at 9.30 they telephoned my husband to say they were bringing him home. I thought it was silly actually. He wasn't really ill. The minute he got home he sat down and started eating his lunch. My husband was fed up about it – he was off already because he was ill. That is the reason why we thought that [child] had decided to be unwell – because he knew that someone was at home. I thought it was totally unnecessary for the school to send him home.

Accounts by other mothers were also critical of the speed at which some school staff responded to minor illness episodes. The competence of school staff, like that of mothers, was measured and judged in view of the way they reacted to illness in schools. Again, school staff, like mothers, often face a 'no win' situation – if they acted promptly to reports of illness they faced criticism but if they waited they could also face parental disapproval. Mothers and school staff walked a 'tightrope' attempting to balance the practical problems associated with illness management while, at the same time, needing to be perceived as acting in the best possible interests of the sick child, other children and their parents. Teachers might face criticism from parents while parents feared the censure of school staff. The following accounts demonstrate some of the difficulties school staff faced in decision making with regard to illness episodes and the way in which their action was perceived by parents.

I think the teacher she is with goes a little bit overboard. I think it was just the case that she mentioned she had earache – she [the teacher] is straight on the phone. She seems to hit the panic button straight away. [The childminder] thought it was ridiculous having her home. She was as right as rain within half an hour. I thought it was a bit over the top.

They do tend to act a bit quick. It was a wasted day off school really. He wasn't poorly. Perhaps he just complained of tummy ache – they seem to be quick to send them home.

One child was sent home from school after having an accident, but in this instance school staff were criticised for under-reacting.

They [school staff] seem very lacking in – well, first aid training. I was not pleased with the way the school handled it. It was at least half an hour later when they rang me. They said it was just a little accident. It was a very bad accident – his sight is still affected.

Occasionally children were kept off school simply because their mother feared that if they sent their child into school they would be sent home.

It does sound dreadful [but] . . . If I had sent him they would have sent him home. They have before.

A situation which was likely to cause decision making difficulties for mothers and school staff alike was when a child was suspected of exaggerating or feigning illness symptoms. The children in the sample were aged 6–7 years and there has been little research on feigning illness in this age group; indeed the participation of children in the illness process has attracted little research attention. Prout (1988) explains that this gap in the literature occurs as a result of a widely perceived assumption that children:

. . . remained passive recipients of health care rather than active participants in the process of sickness. Second, only the most basic acknowledgement was made to the importance of children's age as a feature salient to the meaning of child health and illness.

Age, then, is perceived by Prout as a crucial factor in the process whereby children negotiate with parents and teachers in the adoption of a 'sick role'. In Prout's work the tendency to feign illness was linked with a particular stage within the childhood 'career', that is, the transition from primary to secondary school. The children in his sample were aged 10–11

years. Research focusing on younger children and their health
care suggests that in preschool children, neither the inclination
nor the ability to feign illness had developed. Mayall (1986),
drawing from mothers' accounts, concluded:

> An important feature of the mothers' interpretation of the
> symptoms is their belief in the naivety of the young child's
> behaviour. These bodily and psychological symptoms are
> seen as the involuntary reaction of the child to the experience
> of feeling unwell. As an adult, one may feel a collection of
> changes or symptoms in oneself could mean various things:
> the onset of illness, reaction to stress, unwillingness to face
> the day's events; and for oneself there remains the question
> whether to become ill, to adopt the sick role, to succumb,
> or whether to soldier on, to work one's way through it.
> Judging from mothers' accounts, they believe that there is
> no such decision making in small children.

Hence, the child's age seems to be important and the stage the
child has reached in its childhood 'career'; however, the matter of
feigning sickness and adopting a sick role may not simply be one
concerning the child's developmental stage but may relate to
the practical implications of feigning. As Prout points out, and as
mentioned earlier in this chapter, for the school age child adopting a sick role might imply a major change in the day's routine,
which may not be the case for a preschool age child. The sick
role may imply more attention or pampering but also, and
perhaps most crucially, a day off school. For Prout, feigning
was a symptom of the transition from primary to secondary
school which symbolized a 'rite of passage' from childhood to
adult life and the latter implied the development of characteristics of stoicism. The children in our sample did not face this
transition – the day-to-day demands of schooling or more
particular worries about school were sufficient to bring
accomplished acting skills to the fore. The following account,
by a mother who was called from work to bring her child home
from school, demonstrates the way in which a young child
could take an active role in negotiating a sickness 'state'.

> I wasn't convinced it was genuine to be honest. [in the
> morning] she was crying saying her throat hurt her – I
> looked at her throat, it was all right. I said she was going

[to school], so, I said if anything was wrong the teacher could ring me. The teacher had seen through her – she had told her, but she had told her to get on with her work. So, she worked on the dinnertime supervisor who is more gullible. I have a sneaky feeling she doesn't like PE. It is Monday afternoon PE. She was as right as ninepence by the time we got to the car. If it happens again I am going in to see. [This was the second consecutive Monday afternoon that the child had been sent home.]

Deciding whether a child was feigning was sometimes difficult. Occasionally, the child presented with minor symptoms and it was difficult for mothers and school staff to decide whether the child was ill or whether to give the child the benefit of the doubt. In some cases this decision was very specific to the child, as some children regularly presented themselves as 'ill'.

They called me from school. She might have complained in the morning of tummy ache but I didn't think she was that poorly. We quite often get that in the morning.

She was rather jubilant when she found out that she wasn't going to school. She was just a bit mangey – she was flushed – she was all right. They are quite cute.

Deciding whether a child was feigning or not was not just a problem for working mothers. In the same way as deciding whether a child was well enough for school, judging whether a child was 'pretending' was perceived as a matter of maternal competence. If a child did manage to fool school staff and its mother but was later found to be well, this might mean that the child would be disciplined. Indeed, some home nursing strategies were deliberately adopted for mainly punitive reasons; for example, a frequent justification given for keeping children indoors was 'if they can't go to school they can't play out' – no work, no play. The following account is taken from an interview with a non-working mother.

He was quiet when I collected him from school but as soon as I got out of the grounds he was all right. I wasn't bothered about them ringing me up [from school] but when I found out he was all right I wasn't chuffed. . . . He won't be doing it again.

Sometimes children were suspected of feigning or their symptoms were regarded as minor, but nevertheless they were kept at home 'just to be on the safe side'.

Well, he just said he had earache and he didn't wish to go to school the following day! That was it! I kept him off just to make sure that nothing came of it.

She was sent home on the Thursday. I left her home the next day in case she started with it again.

During the monitoring phase, there were 13 episodes in which 'worry about burdening teachers' was the first reason given by mothers for keeping their child away from school and it was mentioned in a further 16 episodes as a second reason. In 22 episodes the child had been sent home from school or the child had been advised to stay at home by the teacher (three mothers mentioned this as a second reason for keeping their child off). In addition there was a range of other reasons mothers gave for keeping their child away from school, many of which related to the environment or conditions in school, in addition to the nature of the child's illness. Children with sickness and/or diarrhoea were frequently absent because of fears of spreading disease, but also because of the practical problems these ailments could cause in school.

He said his stomach was a bit sick. I didn't want him going into school and puking all over the class.

Well, I thought if she was wanting to run to the toilet . . .

It was more convenient. I didn't want him throwing up at school.

Because it was contagious. I told the teacher and she said keep him off.

He wouldn't have been much good and he would have been passing germs on – consideration for others.

Occasionally, the school curriculum or activities in school were given as reasons for keeping children off school. School trips were mentioned both as reasons for keeping a child off and for sending a child back sooner than might otherwise have been the case after an illness episode. Some mothers expressed worries about their child missing school work while others expressed an opposing view.

> Well, he didn't want to go and he wasn't missing anything on that day so I let him stay off.

> It worried me that he was missing so much. I didn't want him falling behind but there was nothing I could do.

Many mothers had other reasons for keeping the child off which were too varied to classify but included, for example, acting on the advice of the GP or in a few cases the mother herself didn't feel well enough to take the child down to school, or a brother or sister was ill so the child's otherwise minor symptoms led in these particular circumstances to school absence.

Because there was such a wide variety of reasons it was not possible to determine whether mothers in paid employment were more likely to keep their child off school for a particular type of reason. There was no evidence that maternal employment had any effect on the likelihood of children being sent home from school by staff. Mothers at home may have perceived that they were easier to contact, which may have meant that they were in a better position to negotiate in 'doubtful' illness situations; if a child seemed slightly off colour then school staff would be able to contact them, requesting that the child be taken home. This may not have been an option for working mothers.

It may also have been the case that school staff were more reluctant to send children home if they knew that the mother was working because the mother might be difficult to contact. It may have been that in a few cases, irrespective of maternal employment, staff considered that the child would receive better treatment if s/he remained in school, but we had no interview evidence to support these speculations. Some working mothers were relatively easy to reach at their work whilst mothers who were at home may have been difficult to contact. Not being at work would not guarantee that the mother would spend all day actually in her home, as the following account explains.

> We had a disaster – [child] fell on the slippy floor in the toilets and banged his head. They were ringing me all

morning from school and I wasn't there, I was at work. Anyway I got there about a quarter past one . . . we ended up staying the night at St James' [Hospital]. I felt really bad. I thought the one time they needed me they couldn't get hold of me. But then you can't really sit by the phone all day, not going out, waiting for them to ring you. [Mother working part time.]

Overall, it seemed that whether mothers were in paid work or not, they justified keeping their child off school in the same kinds of way. Were there any other ways in which the constraints of the mothers' work impinged on decision making in relation to school attendance? Accounts gathered during interviews at Phase II suggest that once the mother had decided that the child was to be absent from school, maternal employment made no significant difference to the ways in which mothers justified this decision.

When explaining why they had decided to keep their child off school, mothers were unlikely to mention work related issues; such issues might well affect when a child was absent (for example, if a child had an ongoing condition then a day off school might coincide with a mother's day off work) but would not explain why the child was absent. Work related issues were much more likely to be used to justify and explain why a child was not absent from school and at Phase II of the research we did not follow up every episode of illness but just those that had led to school absence. However, there was some evidence to suggest that if mothers worked fulltime their child was likely to have considerably less school absence than a child whose mother was at home. The following section describes these differences between groups and speculates about why they might have occurred.

NUMBER OF ABSENCE EPISODES, LENGTH OF EPISODES AND MOTHERS' EMPLOYMENT

During the monitoring stage of the project, the length of individual episodes and the number of episodes were recorded and overall absence was calculated. The length of the individual episodes were recorded in relation to the mother's work status at the time of the episode.

Chapter 6 describes the types of illnesses which led to school absence during the monitoring phase of the research. It is sufficient to mention at this point that most of the illnesses were self-limiting, that is, the children mainly recovered without intervention. In addition, the illnesses were usually fairly minor and of relatively short duration.

The mean length of school absence per illness episode was about two and a half school days (2.51 days). When the length of episodes for children whose mothers were in work was compared with that for children whose mothers were at home, there was very little difference between the two groups, with the average length of episode being 2.52 and 2.56 days respectively. However, the mean length of episode for the children whose mothers worked fulltime was less, closer to two days absence per episode (2.04). However, the difference was not found to be significant in statistical terms.

Similar differences were found in the number of illness episodes over the monitoring period, with children of mothers working fulltime having, on average, the fewest episodes. Again the differences between the groups did not attain a level of statistical significance.

We then compared children of mothers in the three groups in terms of their overall absence, that is, the number of episodes multiplied by the length of those episodes. In order to compare the three groups in terms of total absence it was necessary to select the mothers who had maintained the same work status throughout the monitoring period. Some mothers changed their work status during the course of the research. Several mothers moved into the labour market whilst others moved out and their behaviour during illness episodes may have been affected by these moves. Hence, for comparisons of total absence we compared those mothers who were in fulltime, part-time or no paid employment at both the beginning and end of the monitoring period. There were 105 of these mothers.

Over the 25 school weeks of monitoring, children whose mothers were at home had an average of 6.67 days absent; children whose mothers worked part-time took 5.35 days; and children whose mothers worked fulltime took an average of only 3.00 days. The difference between the groups was statistically significant.

How can we explain these differences? Were children of mothers who worked fulltime less ill? If so, why should this be? Does the explanation lie in clinical factors – for whatever reasons, did these children have less disease? Or did emotional or psychological factors come into play: did children across the groups have the same amount of disease but they and their mothers responded to this disease in different ways? Or were social factors and practical constraints (particularly constraints associated with maternal employment) influencing the way that children and mothers responded to illness? A further consideration was whether decisions about disease and illness and those about school attendance were the same thing, or did quite different factors come into play; that is, did mothers working fulltime send their children into school ill or did mothers at home keep their children off for 'trivial' reasons? Alternatively, was the child in the former case regarded as 'well enough for school' while in the latter perceived as 'ill'? Are none of these explanations sufficient to explain the differences in attendance behaviour?

A complicating factor is that it is the fulltime workers who are distinctive. Part-time workers seem on our evidence to be rather more similar to mothers at home. Are, then, the reasons for the differences between the groups more subtle? Are the decisions concerning the child's illness and its severity *and* the decision about school attendance related but compounded by a whole range of considerations of a clinical, practical and emotional nature? Could it be the case that both childhood illness and school attendance are open to negotiation? If so, are there any circumstances in which the consequences of such a seemingly 'elastic' decision making process are likely to be of detriment to the child, its mother, other family members, other school children or school staff?

ILLNESS AND SCHOOL ATTENDANCE
– OPEN TO NEGOTIATION?

There are, then, various possible explanations as to why children of mothers in fulltime work seem to have less school absence. First, there is the possible explanation that children of mothers that work fulltime are 'less ill'. In this context, how can we define what 'less ill' means? Is it possible to measure degrees of illness or is illness a subjective experience rather than something that can be objectively gauged? There is a considerable literature which distinguishes between the terms 'disease' and 'illness'; in short, the term disease is used to refer to the physical changes in the body which cause some form of malfunction, while illness is the experience of that change. Hence, it is possible to have a disease and not feel ill or to have feelings of illness where there is no attributable disease present. From this literature it seems that illness is 'negotiable' in that the experience of disease by individuals is likely to differ. Even if the severity of a condition could be measured with any degree of precision, there is no measure of the way that any given child experiences a given level of disease severity. Emotionality may differ between children: some children may be more stoical whilst others may 'make a fuss' and this behaviour may in turn affect the child's experience of the disease. Further, the child's experience of symptoms may relate to the child's expectations of getting a day off school or increased attention from parents or teachers. The 'agenda' may be different for those children whose mothers are in paid work. For the child, clinical, emotional and social or practical factors may all contribute to the child's experience of the illness 'state'. Further, mothers may perceive a child's complaints of illness in different ways and this inter-pretation may depend on several factors: practical constraints, beliefs about illness and the clinical manifestations of disease. Some of these factors may throw light upon the problem of explaining differences in behaviour across the groups.

FROM THE CLINICAL TO THE PRACTICAL

It is worth repeating that most of the conditions leading to absence were both fairly minor and 'self-limiting'; school attendance or absence were unlikely in themselves to affect the eventual clinical outcome for the child in terms of recovery. Many minor viral conditions, for example, 'run their course' and interventions by doctors or adopting particular home nursing strategies may provide symptomatic relief and thereby reduce any distress the child is experiencing but do not 'cure' the condition and are unlikely to affect the duration of the illness.

If the clinical nature of the disease itself does not determine whether the child should or should not attend school, the issue of school attendance may become more negotiable. In some of the more extreme cases of coughs or colds clinical factors alone could determine a particular course of action: if a child was breathless, feverish and delirious, vomiting or dizzy then the decision regarding whether or not the child was ill and the decision regarding school attendance would be straightforward. In milder cases, the child's reaction to the disease or other considerations might be more likely to come into play.

It is important to recognize that decisions about illness – the negotiation of the sick role by the child, mother and school staff – may not necessarily be the same as the negotiation of school attendance. For example, the decision whether or not to attend school from the child's point of view may not relate to the feelings of illness at all; minor symptoms may present a means of dodging school. Mothers' accounts demonstrate that clinical considerations form only part of the decision making process; being seen to be a 'bad mother' may tip the balance in favour of absence but may be unrelated to the perceived severity of the child's disease. From the class teacher's point of view an ill child may pose a threat to other children in the form of infection but there are, in some cases, classroom management problems associated with having an ill child in school which do not relate in any way to the physical welfare of any of the children. As the following account demonstrates, the problem of 'managing' an ill child was sometimes a matter of negotiation between the mother and class teacher; the child's physical condition alone could not resolve the issue of school attendance.

> [The doctor] said, as far as he was concerned she could go back but it was up to the teachers whether they could put up with her. Well I said I was going to keep her off for the rest of the week but the teacher said she could cope with it. They are used to it, it has happened before. She has been like that for years now so you just have to put up with it. [child with asthma]

In conditions such as coughs and colds (the most common cause of school absence) where there is a considerable range of severity, decisions concerning school attendance are fairly elastic; below a certain level of severity, deciding at which point a condition becomes 'serious' enough to merit a day off school is open to question. From the clinical point of view, if school attendance does not adversely affect the course of the disease and the child is not distressed by the condition (that is, if the child does not experience 'illness', and this may depend on the emotionality of the child as well as the severity of the condition) then, as far as that child's health is concerned, there is no reason for the child to be at home.

We have asserted that for coughs and colds, decision making in relation to both the adoption by the child of a 'sick role' and school attendance may be largely negotiable. Are gastroenteric conditions – 'tummy troubles' – less so? If a child was likely to have an attack of vomiting or diarrhoea, they were frequently perceived by mothers to be best away from the classroom – both because the conditions were frequently reported as being distressing for the child and because they were perceived to be infectious as well as posing practical problems for teachers. However, for vomiting and diarrhoea there was still some room for negotiation; the stage at which the illness ended was indistinct and the decision about when this occurred may have been less concerned with clinical factors than with social or psychological ones. Was the child 'better' a few hours after the last attack of vomiting, after the child had had 'three good meals', 'a good night's rest', just 'managed to keep something down', or when the child was 'eating normally' or had 'got her colour back'?

Concern about spreading infection in the case of contagious diseases is a quite separate but important issue in the negotiation of illness and school attendance. An account quoted earlier in this chapter suggests that one of the reasons schools are seen as a source of illness is that certain parents send their children into school with communicable diseases. The diseases the mother mentioned were certainly infectious – chickenpox and measles – but deciding whether a child with a 'runny nose' should be isolated is not so simple. Spreading infection or 'catching' disease are as much psychological as clinical phenomena. Fear of disease is often only partly rational and does not relate to the actual transmission of bacterial or viral infection (this issue is discussed more fully in Chapter 5). While some mothers regarded coughs and colds as infectious, others did not.

The following sections explore in more detail the clinical, emotional and social aspects of the decision making process. None of these aspects alone explains why it was the case that some children were off school less than others but together, weighing in each of the factors at different stages in the decision making process, they do help us to make sense of the process and its results.

MATERNAL EMPLOYMENT, ILLNESS SEVERITY AND THE NEGOTIATION OF THE SICK ROLE

Mothers' accounts demonstrate that there was a fairly large degree of negotiation in terms of what was to 'count' as illness. For some a cold was 'normal'; for others it was an illness.

I thought it was just a normal cold – just a runny nose.

Could it be that the negotiation of illness and decisions about school attendance relate to the mother's work status? That is, that children of fulltime mothers might be deemed to be 'not ill' where the same condition and degree of severity in children of non-working mothers might be seen as meriting the illness 'label'. If so, could this explain the differences between the two groups in terms of school attendance? First then, how dependent is the negotiation of illness on the nature and severity of the disease?

School absence and disease severity

Although it was not possible to measure disease severity with any degree of accuracy in the absence of a clinical examination, we were able, as part of the Phase II questionnaire, to incorporate a rough measure of severity by means of a series of closed questions about the child's symptoms and the functional effects of the disease on the child – that is, the degree to which the condition affected the child's normal daily life. In the case of coughs and colds the 'severity' questions were developed by a team of social scientists and paediatricians (Wyke et al., 1991) and have been used and tested in earlier studies (Wyke and Hewison, 1991; Clarke and Hewison, 1991).

The reason for incorporating this measure was to test whether children with more or less severe coughs were perceived as being more or less ill by different groups and whether differences in behaviour could be accounted for by differing degrees of severity. In short, if children of mothers working fulltime were absent from school, were their coughs and colds 'worse', that is, of greater severity, than those of children whose mothers were at home? Putting it another way, was there any evidence that children of working mothers were more likely to attend school with 'slight' or trivial coughs? Were mothers at home more likely to keep their children off with these more trivial conditions?

Although a measure of severity was used in an attempt to assess the importance of 'clinical' factors in the decision making process, as a clinical measure it had its shortcomings. The most obvious problem was that there was no physical examination of the child at the time of the illness episode. Additionally, the measure included questions relating to the functional outcomes of the disease and these may not be wholly clinical in nature. For example, loss of appetite might be less a clinical than an emotional matter. One mother, for example, claimed that her child was always 'off her food' and that this state of affairs was 'nothing new'; appetite, for this child, was not simply determined by the presence of disease but may have been partly due to emotional or personality factors. Hence, even questions which ostensibly measured clinical factors also took into account the effects of disease on the child. A third potential problem with the severity measure was that it depended on the mothers' perceptions of the illness after the event and although the questions were precise and closed, it is possible that mothers sought to justify their actions in relation to school attendance or doctor consultation by exaggerating or 'down-playing' as appropriate the reported clinical manifestations of disease. In an attempt to minimize this, the 'severity' questions were administered before those relating to behaviour.

The severity of the illness as we measured it did not explain the group differences in school attendance for the 97 episodes of cough and cold. The children whose mothers were in fulltime work did not have a higher average severity score than children from the other groups. Indeed, the mean severity of the episode across the three groups – children of mothers working fulltime, part-time or at home – were very similar.

It did not, therefore, seem that mothers who worked fulltime adopted a different threshold of severity when deciding whether or not to keep their child off school: their children did not apparently have to have 'worse' coughs before they were kept off school. To avoid the possibility that a small number of families with a large number of episodes each had biased the results, the analysis was repeated using only the first episode for each family, but this produced the same result.

One possible means of reconciling the different sets of findings on absence and severity was suggested from an inspection of the distributions of severity scores in the three work status groups. It was very noticeable that the range of severity scores exhibited by children of non-working mothers (6 to 105) was much higher than that seen in the children of fulltime workers (30 to 84); that is, some of the episodes seen in the former had been very trivial, while others had been very serious respiratory conditions, often severe bouts of asthma. Formal statistical tests were carried out comparing the amount of variability in the two groups (Levene, 1960) and despite the relatively small number of episodes ($n = 12$) in the fulltime group, the result did approach statistical significance.

It seems likely that different explanations are required for the apparent shortfall of trivial and serious episodes in the children of fulltime workers. Mothers at home may have been more inclined to keep their children off school for trivial illnesses; and since episodes were identified in the study from school absence, trivial episodes that did not lead to absence would not have been detected. As for serious episodes, it is most unlikely that episodes generating scores in the sixties or above would not have led to school absence so the most plausible explanation here is that mothers of children prone to such episodes, e.g. those with bad asthma, had decided they could not take on a fulltime job for that very reason. Both of these processes would contribute, via different chains of cause and effect, to reducing the overall amount of school absence in children of fulltime workers, while being consistent with no difference in the mean severity of illness episodes leading to absence in the different work status groups.

Another piece of evidence to support this speculation comes from the Phase I interviews when mothers were asked whether their child had any recurring illnesses. Proportionately fewer of the children whose mothers worked fulltime were said to have a recurrent illness although this trend was not strong enough to reach statistical significance on the numbers available.

It did seem, then, that for coughs and colds there were some differences in the pattern – though not the average level – of illness severity between the groups. Unfortunately we had no comparable measure of severity for vomiting and diarrhoea or for the other common conditions that afflicted the study children.

It could be argued that vomiting and diarrhoea present symptoms of a type which lead to more straightforward symptom related decision making. If this were true, then negotiation of the illness state of the kind envisaged for coughs and colds could not take place for gastroenteric conditions. Thus we might have expected fewer coughs and colds amongst the absence episodes of children of mothers working fulltime, but no difference between groups for the less negotiable conditions such as diarrhoea and vomiting.

No pattern of this kind was found. Children of mothers working fulltime seemed to have less illness across all conditions. How could this be explained? It could be that the children of mothers working fulltime were different from those in the 'at home' group in other respects. It could be that maternal employment was confounded by socio-economic factors and this could possibly account for a different distribution of diseases across groups. This was not the case; although there were slightly more fulltime workers in higher socio-economic groups, socio-economic factors did not seem to be associated with illness distribution.

Could it be, then, that negotiation of illness in the case of diarrhoea and vomiting is less concerned with the severity of the condition and more related to the duration of the illness? For example, if the last attack of vomiting was on a Sunday evening, then it would be open to question whether the child was still 'ill' enough on Monday not to attend school. We can only speculate, because our research data only describe what happened when a child was absent from school; we have no direct evidence about the decision making process during illness if it did not result in school absence.

Emotionality and the negotiation of the illness state

If the severity of the illness only partially explains attendance behaviour, can other non-clinical factors shed light on the decision making process? Could it be that both children and mothers in the different groups react to disease in different ways and that what is 'ill' for one child and possibly also that child's mother is just slightly 'off colour' or 'under the weather' for someone else? Could it be that children of 'at home' mothers are more likely to 'make a fuss', either because they perceive more severe symptoms or in the belief that they will be taken more seriously by their mothers or in the expectation of a day off? Children of mothers working fulltime might behave more stoically for all the opposite reasons; in the face of minor symptoms it might make more sense for them not to 'overplay' symptoms as a day off school may not be 'on the cards'. The sickness 'agenda' might be different for the two groups.

The question of how distressed the child was or seemed may be important and possibly offers a partial explanation of why some children may have been deemed 'ill' and were therefore absent from school whilst others with similar symptoms of disease were not regarded as ill.

There has been some research which suggests that the mother's work status may be related in some way to the 'emotionality' of the child or the way that children react to disease. The correlation was, however, said to be 'slender' and clearly the direction of causation is open to question. As Campbell (1978) notes, 'Does the mother's working lead to a child's stoic self-report, or do mothers of less emotional children feel more free to work?' As children were not interviewed as part of our research, the possibility that children of fulltime working mothers are more stoical in the face of symptoms of disease remains an intriguing suggestion which could not be tested.

To conclude this section, the child, mother, school staff and other family members could all participate in the negotiation of a child's sick role and the decision regarding school attendance. Disease severity, psychological factors and practical circumstances could all contribute to the interpretation of the 'illness state' and the decision regarding absence. None of these factors taken in isolation could satisfactorily explain why children of mothers working fulltime had less absence and the causality question touched upon above also remains unresolved. It might be the case that children of fulltime working mothers are 'less ill' because their mothers work; but it could also be suggested that children who are 'less ill' allow their mothers the opportunity to seek fulltime employment opportunities.

Before concluding this chapter on schools and childhood illness episodes we will briefly describe some of the other ways in which schools were found to impinge on the illness decision making process.

THE RETURN TO SCHOOL AFTER AN ILLNESS EPISODE

Just as the decision concerning school absence was mainly justified in mothers' accounts by reference to clinical factors or other characteristics of the 'illness', so too was the decision about the return to school after that illness was over. However, the latter decision seemed to offer increased scope for the role of practical or circumstantial considerations. Again, the decision making process actively involved the child, other family members and school staff as well as the mother herself. Unlike the decision regarding absence, work related factors were used to justify the decision about the child's return to school and in particular were used to explain the timing of the return. In other respects mothers in and out of paid employment gave similar reasons for sending their children back to school.

The most frequent justification for sending a child back to school was that the child had completely recovered or that there were no apparent signs of disease. This was the first reason given for a return to school in 53% of the episodes of illness followed up during the monitoring stage; and where a second reason was given, the child's recovery was mentioned on a further 23 occasions. Sometimes mothers claimed that although symptoms had not totally abated, they were less severe and that the child was – despite residual signs of disease – now 'fit' for school. Making this kind of distinction was particularly common for coughs. In 30% of episodes, less severe symptoms or the child being 'less ill' were mentioned to justify the decision to send the child back to school at a particular time and these were given as a second reason in 16 episodes. The child being 'back to normal' or 'less ill' were both relative terms and depended on the mother's particular knowledge of the child. Children were frequently described as 'running around', 'full of energy – driving me mad'. A change in appetite or sleep patterns also signified recovery – if a child 'had had a good meal' or 'slept right through' their illness was judged to be less severe. The following accounts show how mothers made decisions regarding their children's recovery and return to school – again the two decisions were not synonymous and again the child could be active in the process.

> I think if they get their sleep they can cope the next day. Well he seemed to have had a good sleep and he was bored silly.

> She had her colour back and she was back to herself.

> She just wasn't coughing as much.

> She ate her tea and she seemed all right and she wasn't barking or anything this morning.

> Well, he was all right. Jumping about and everything else and eating.

Occasionally length of absence was determined by advice from the GP (this was only mentioned in 3% of episodes). The child wanting to go back, being bored or missing something at school also prompted the decision to send the child back to school.

> Well, I thought she seemed a lot better and she was missing things at school that were important – rehearsals for the Christmas play. I probably sent her back a bit early in a way but she wanted to go back. But she wasn't 100%.

> Well, he still isn't right but I felt he had just had too much time off.

Occasionally mothers mentioned their work commitments as a reason for sending their child back to school, but this was unusual. The first of the following accounts was taken from an interview with a mother who worked fulltime. The child had been absent for just a morning after being up in the night vomiting. The mother was asked when she had decided that the child could go back to school.

At lunchtime. Through necessity. Really she should have had the whole day off, but she was fit enough to survive the afternoon. I didn't want to look after her that afternoon. I have to go to work and it really isn't that flexible. There is no cover at all.

Well, to be quite honest he went back Thursday because there was no-one to look after him.

She didn't look too bad really and I thought she might as well go as me losing all my wage. That is a big factor in it.

Sometimes home circumstances or school practices determined the time the child returned to school. In the following account, taken from an interview with a mother who was at home, these circumstances led to a more prolonged absence.

Thursday he was back to normal. Really he might have been well enough Wednesday but I was going out so I thought I'd have to take him with me because the slightest thing and they ring you up and I wouldn't have been here.

Sometimes the return to school was not a matter for negotiation with the child – the following account is from an interview with a mother that was at home.

He was all right. Usually I don't decide – should I send them? I send them unless they feel worse!

In about a third of the episodes (34%) the child was receiving medication after the return to school. In 22% of these cases medicines were sent into school with the child, while in the remaining episodes medication was administered at home. There were differing views about whether or not school staff should or would give out medicines. Some children were on regular medication and parents depended on school staff to administer it. According to some parents, school staff were happy for the children to take medication into school, but others expressed an opposite opinion. These views did not seem to relate to the school the child attended. The following accounts describe some of these attitudes:

The teacher looks after it, but he knows how to use it himself [inhaler]. The teacher is happy to do that. They are very good at school – I am pleased with the concern they have for the children.

The headteacher gives them medicine. They are very good about that, provided you give clear instructions.

I don't send them. Schools don't like to administer any sort of medicine.

It was just night and morning. Besides they do not like dishing out medicines. Their policy is, if a child is on medicines they are not well enough to be in school, which I tend to agree with.

If you send medicines, really and truly they should be at home. There could be negligence. If you need medication you should be at home. It is a very grey area.

Sometimes, what were perceived as 'school policies' regarding the distribution of medicines led mothers to restrict the use of medication. In most episodes this did not cause any problems but occasionally it meant that the dosage and frequency of prescribed drugs were altered.

I managed to give him it at home. It was supposed to be four times a day. He was actually having it three times, but it was OK.

It was supposed to be four times a day. It is difficult, isn't it? I don't like sending medicines into school. She probably didn't get the right doses [just having it at home] – I don't know whether it was important. I don't like sending medicine, they might think that if they are taking medicine they shouldn't be there.

I couldn't give him the lunchtime one because he was in school. He hasn't completed the course ... You aren't allowed to have it in school. I don't agree with them having it in school – they could get mixed up.

In around two thirds of the episodes, mothers said that they had contacted school about the illness. In 58 episodes (20%) the school had got in touch with the mother; either the child was sent home from school or teachers telephoned home or kept the mother back after school to discuss the child's health.

It may seem from some of the above accounts that mothers frequently felt dissatisfied with the staff at their child's school because of the way they handled illness episodes. This was not in fact the case. At the third stage of the research mothers were asked how satisfied they felt with the way the school dealt with child health matters. They were asked to rate their satisfaction on a 1–5 scale. Of the 124 mothers who answered these questions only 20 expressed reservations: nine mothers were uncertain, nine said they were fairly unsatisfied and two very unsatisfied with the way that schools handled children's illnesses. Despite the fact that mothers, on the whole, said they were satisfied with the school, when they were asked to explain their rating a few more mothers made negative comments about the school. This may have been a problem with the way some mothers interpreted the scale. For some the term 'quite satisfied' implied a positive view of the school while for others it was a qualified view meaning 'less than wholly satisfied' and as such expressed a negative view. One hundred and sixty seven responses were recorded (some mothers gave two responses): 37 were classified as negative comments about the school and the rest positive. Satisfaction with the school did not relate to maternal employment: of the 37 negative comments, 29 were made by employed and eight by non-employed mothers. Fulltime mothers were less likely to say they were 'very satisfied' with school as compared with those mothers in part-time work or at home but the trend was not statistically significant. Nine mothers were specifically critical about the speed at which school staff contacted parents.

> All they seem to do is send them home. I go to pick him up and he is as right as a bobbin when he gets home. I get sick of it.

However, the negative comments about the speed with which schools contacted parents in cases of illness were far outweighed by positive comments about this (45 comments).

Well, they generally point it out to you if your child has been off it during the day – which is helpful because children are up and down and you might not have noticed in the morning.

Working mothers were more likely to be critical about the speed at which children were sent home from school although the numbers were too small for the finding to be statistically significant. Of the nine mothers who mentioned this, eight were in paid work and only one at home.

We will end this chapter with a few of the very positive comments about schools. School staff, like mothers, are expected to perform a balancing act attempting to weigh and juggle the many considerations that are involved in illness negotiation. In some cases, like mothers, they were criticized for their choices, but mostly it was recognized by mothers that these choices were by no means simple and that teachers were acting in what a parent earlier described as a 'grey area'. Little wonder, then, that their choices and actions did not please all parents all the time. Their relative success can be gauged by the fact that they did please many of the parents at least some of the time.

I will be sick when [child] leaves the school in the summer. The headteacher is wonderful. She always has time for you, she has been really good to me.

They [school staff] are just absolutely great. I have never had any trouble with anything. They are very understanding and caring people.

5

The sick child – who cares?

The first section of this chapter describes the arrangements made for providing care. It addresses issues relating to the quality of care and considers whether the standard of care for children of working mothers was less good than that provided by mothers who were at home. We look at the individuals who provided child health care and consider whether working mothers could be said to 'palm off' their sick children while they went out to work. Less contentiously, what types of family arrangements did mothers make to ensure that their child was well cared for during illness episodes? We also examine the ways in which families paid for child care during illness episodes: whether there was cash payment for care or whether mothers faced other indirect costs. We assess the contribution of various family members, including grandparents and other members of the extended family, to child health care and we consider how the burden of responsibility for arranging and actually providing care is shared within families. We look in particular at the contribution of the child's father to child health care. The final sections of the chapter consider the ways in which mothers rate the help they receive from other family members and their satisfaction with the arrangements they have made for the care of their sick child.

For a working mother the decision to go into work while her child is ill implies a decision about the care of her child during the time she is working. For a mother who is at home during the day the decisions surrounding the care of her child may be more straightforward as the mother herself would generally be in a position to provide most of the care. However, mothers at home and those in paid work share some of the problems associated with caring for a sick child. A child's illness may mean that both mother and child are virtually housebound. It may be difficult for a mother to care for a sick child in addition to meeting the usual demands of running a home and caring for other family members. A mother may be unable to get out to the shops or chemists; collecting brothers and sisters from school might involve either taking the sick child out, finding alternative care at the beginning and end of the school day, or making other arrangements for the care of siblings. The following accounts demonstrate that such problems applied irrespective of maternal employment.

> Getting the Christmas shopping was a nightmare. I couldn't get out. Luckily he was well over the few Christmas days.

> I had to send [her brother] in a taxi down to school because I had no one to take him down. My mum would have come but she has quite a long way to come.

> Being tied. Not being able to get up and down to school to get the other kids. You can't leave a child ill at home while you get the others.

> You can't get out. I have to put them in the car, it is the only way you can do. My sister, she has kiddies, and my mother works, [they] can't really come if they have got owt like chickenpox because they might catch it. They would come if I was desperate.

If a mother had to leave her home, either to go to work or to meet other commitments associated with looking after her family, it was necessary to arrange, often at very short notice, reliable, cheap and quality care for her sick child. The ideal solution might be that proposed by the former Prime Minister, Mrs Thatcher, in a speech we quoted in Chapter 1:

> But no matter how hard any woman planned to combine work and the family, it was impossible to do everything oneself. You have to seek reliable help, or what my mother would have called a treasure.

But who are these 'treasures'? Do all mothers have access to them? The word treasure suggests something very dear or of value. In reality, the person is likely to be a relative, friend, neighbour or paid helper whose services are provided cheaply or free, despite their high value. Is there a pool or 'treasure chest' of low cost, high quality help available to mothers?

Further, during children's illness episodes the need for very special caring qualities arises. Would even a close relative be prepared to step in to provide not only substitute child care but possibly nursing services too? The tasks associated with nursing children during illness episodes are more than mothers would normally expect of paid childminders or school staff. The following account describes the nature of one of the caring tasks necessary during an episode of diarrhoea – escorting a sick grandchild to the lavatory.

> She just kept saying, 'come on gran' and she was off to the lav. Watery diarrhoea . . . I have never known anybody going oftener. She was going pretty reg.

Even if the nature of the child's complaint did not imply unpleasant duties for the carer, it was necessary for the carer to be prepared to take responsibility for the ill child. Again this was not generally expected of paid helpers, particularly while a child was distressed by the illness.

> The only thing that makes it easier to deal with is that the childminder is willing to have her. We [both parents] took a day off and by that time she was more or less over it, so she went to the childminder. . . . We are very lucky that we have got a childminder that is prepared to look after her when she is poorly.

Although neighbours could be drafted in to provide short term child care during school holidays, care during sickness was a more difficult issue. As one of the accounts above notes, it would be unfair to ask for help if the child's condition was possibly infectious, particularly if the carer was old or had children of her own. In the following accounts mothers describe their feelings about leaving their child with their own mothers.

> She is getting old now and is not in very good health herself. So I would have to dash up to get the shopping and get back.

> My mum usually looks after them if they are ill or my sister can come over. It is lucky that I have got quite a lot of family, I have no neighbours that I can rely on.

Mothers, whether in work or not, occasionally had to rely on help during children's illness episodes. Clearly, the amount of help the mother would need would depend on circumstances such as whether or not she was in paid work, the hours and times of day she was working and the number of other children in the family. The quality of the care might depend on a range of factors including the availability of reliable local kin or resources available to pay for help from childminders or nannies. The following section examines these issues of child care needs and resources for providing care.

PALMING CHILDREN OFF?

During the monitoring stage of the research mothers were asked to describe the arrangements made for the provision of care. If more than one person was involved in caring for the sick child this was also noted.

In 84% of episodes of illness the main carer was the mother herself. Hence, in only about a sixth of the episodes was the greater part of care provided by someone else. In the remaining episodes the main carers comprised eight fathers, 21 grandmothers, nine other relatives, four non-relatives and two paid helpers. If the episodes are considered in terms of maternal employment, mothers in paid work were more likely to depend on someone else to provide some care, particularly if the mother worked fulltime. In only two of the episodes where the mother was at home was someone other than the mother the main carer; in these cases the child's maternal grandmother provided care.

Although in 15% of episodes mothers in paid work did rely on other primary carers, they by no means palmed their children off. Where the mother did not provide all of the care herself the child would mainly be left with a close relative, either the child's father, grandmother or aunt, and only very infrequently with neighbours or paid helpers. As the accounts above demonstrate, there would need to be a close relationship with the paid helper or neighbour before the mother would leave her ill child with them. This was for three reasons. First, many mothers assumed that they or close relatives would be the ones their child would most like to be with; second, close relatives were considered to provide the best care;

third, only a trusted friend could be approached and asked to provide, free or at low cost, the kind of care needed by a sick child.

In about a third of episodes, the child was likely to have more than one carer. This 'secondary' care, however, varied in duration depending upon the mothers' needs. In some episodes, the mother would need someone to step in to care for her child for just a few minutes, for example whilst she collected a prescription from the chemists. In other episodes mothers would need others to provide care for several hours whilst they went out to work. If the mother was in paid work it was more likely that there would be more than one carer, although the differences between the groups were not as great as one might expect.

Many mothers, irrespective of work commitments, needed some assistance during children's illness episodes. In 13 episodes non-employed mothers depended on help from others for at least a short time, while in 88 episodes where the mother was in paid work, the child would have more than one carer. In eight episodes (all where the mother was employed) the child had three or more carers. Secondary care was provided by fathers in 26 episodes (9%), grandmothers in 28 episodes (10%), other relatives in 11 episodes, non-relatives in six episodes and paid helpers in three episodes. In all, the child's grandmother was involved in caring either as the first or second carer in 21% of episodes. In 12% of episodes the child's father provided some care.

If we look at the situation from the point of view of individual mothers rather than the episodes of illness, more than half of the mothers (51%) relied on other carers to provide some care on at least one occasion and a quarter of the mothers (25%) relied on the child's grandmother to provide care on at least one occasion. Paid helpers or childminders were mentioned in only five episodes and in all, in only 13 episodes was there any cash payment for care.

Thus, wherever possible mothers themselves provided most of their children's care. When they could not do so, others were drafted in to help. These 'helpers' were mainly close relatives who generally were not paid in cash for their help. What, then, were the feelings of mothers about enlisting relatives to provide largely unpaid help at short notice?

How did mothers discharge their obligations to their relatives and neighbours for the child care and nursing services they provided?

PAYING FOR CARE

While most mothers did not pay directly in cash for child care, many attempted to 'pay' carers in other ways. Some mothers had reciprocal arrangements with relatives, friends and neighbours, who often had children of their own. Despite the fact that mothers sought such help 'only when they were desperate', they still sometimes felt guilty about it. The following accounts indicate some of the many ways mothers came to terms with asking others for help and the variety of methods they used to 'pay' for it.

> Grandma and Grandad looked after him in the afternoon. I didn't think he was so poorly that I couldn't leave him and they were quite willing. . . . [it's not as bad] now as when I first went back to work, at the back of your mind is how to repay them in other ways. We have never paid money but we have to be a bit more thoughtful. I value their time.

> Well you do [feel under obligation] but she wouldn't let you pay. So, I buy cigs and add them to her Christmas box.

> . . . just a nice big flower arrangement.

> I always try to get her something but she doesn't put any pressure on.

> I bought her some flowers. I don't expect her to do it for nothing. I bought her flowers – that is a compromise. They don't refuse those.

> My mum had her at night when I went to work. I do [feel under obligation]. Yes, if I am honest about it I do. I tend to buy things for them when they have had them.

Mothers who gave some kind of 'payment' nevertheless sometimes still felt indebted. Those that did not 'pay' either in cash or gifts sometimes felt guilty, while others considered that help from relatives was a 'right' or that arrangements which involved reciprocity somehow cancelled each other out.

Then on Friday morning Grandma stepped in for me. I felt really guilty because she wasn't well. I was only away for three hours, she wasn't there long. I do feel indebted because when someone has done something for you, you want to do something in return.

It is my mum and she doesn't mind having them.

They are family. That is all.

[re family members] No, I have given them plenty. We work as a unit here. We work together for the good of the family.

I feel I should be here. They [grandparents] do it voluntarily. I felt a bit guilty about leaving him. I've always been here before, but he [child] didn't seem bothered.

As the last of the above accounts demonstrates, mothers were obliged to consider the feelings of their child as well as those of relatives providing care. It was not simply a matter of asking relatives to provide a service at low or no cost. The mother felt that she was asking others to render a service she herself should provide. Some mothers felt that they should stay with their sick child; further, they felt that the child would prefer to be with them.

I didn't like leaving her because she was ill.

Children like to be with their parents when they are ill.

I wouldn't expect my parents to look after them if they were poorly. They need their mothers with them.

There was no evidence that any mother, whether or not she was in paid work, left her child with anyone other than a close relative, trusted friend or neighbour. In most cases mothers tried to be with their children themselves. If this was not possible all the time then the substitute care they arranged was generally provided by a member of the extended family, the most preferred carer being the maternal grandmother.

FAMILY, FRIENDS AND NEIGHBOURS –
THE CARING NETWORK?

One of the questions the study set out to investigate was whether having relatives nearby, potentially available to provide stand-in child care, affected behaviour during illness episodes. For example, was a child more likely to be absent from school if the maternal grandmother lived nearby and was able and willing to provide care at short notice? Further, if mothers did have relatives nearby, were they enlisted to provide care in preference to other potential helpers such as friends and neighbours? Information about the kinds of arrangements made during illness episodes which were dependent on unpaid help from relatives, long-standing friends or neighbourhood networks would then make it possible to speculate about the implications for mothers of losing these 'supports'. This in turn would have implications for the employment opportunities realistically open to mothers and their attitudes towards geographical mobility.

At all three stages in the study mothers were asked about the support that they had obtained from relatives and their feelings about any help they may have received. At the initial and final interviews mothers described the potential sources of help available to them at times of crisis such as during childhood illness episodes. They were asked whether they had family nearby, about the length of time they had resided in their neighbourhood and about who they would be likely to call upon for help during childhood illness episodes.

An account of the areas in which the study was carried out is given in Chapter 2. We anticipated that many of the mothers in these areas would have family living locally, because social and geographical stability were amongst the criteria for choosing areas in the first place. That said, we were surprised at how remarkably stable they were. Most of the mothers interviewed had lived all of their lives in Leeds and had members of their extended family living nearby. In all, 73% of the mothers were born and brought up in the Leeds area and 88% had lived in the city for at least 15 years, which, given the mean age of the respondents, represented much of their adult lives. The length of time that the mothers had lived at their current address appeared relatively short, with the mean length of residence being around three and a half years. However, the sample comprised young mothers and their families, so although new neighbourhood networks may not have been long established, the fact that mothers had local kin living nearby suggests that although families may have moved house as family size increased, many did not move outside the locality and might therefore be able to maintain the network of friends, kin and neighbours established during childhood and early adult life.

Only a very small proportion of the sample had moved into the study areas. Given the small numbers involved, we were unable to look directly at the effects of geographical mobility and the resulting lack of support by local kin and established social networks on mothers' employment and their management of childhood illness episodes. We reasoned instead that if the majority of our sample were found to depend on such support, this would suggest that it did indeed represent a valuable resource for working mothers.

Recasting some of the figures given in an earlier chapter, 80% of the mothers in the sample had members of their own extended family living in or around Leeds and of these, 94% described their family as living 'nearby'. More than half the mothers in the sample (55%) mentioned relatives living less than ten minutes away.

Although it was slightly more common for the mothers rather than fathers to have family living nearby, few fathers had moved away from their 'roots'. Seventy two percent of partners had family living in or around the city, 63% had their own parents living nearby and in 45% of cases the partner's first mentioned relative lived less than ten minutes away.

Of course, having relatives living nearby is not necessarily the same as having relatives available, willing and able to provide support during times of children's illness. Nor is it clear that a relative would automatically be a mother's first choice of carer were she faced with the problem of arranging short term care at short notice.

The findings of our study do seem to indicate that relatives frequently provided help in the form of substitute child care and that relatives, more often than not, were preferred over other potential carers.

GRANDMOTHERS AS HELPERS, CARERS AND MENTORS

For our sample, in 81% of the cases the maternal grandmother was alive at the time of the final interview. Of those grandmothers still living, 85% were said to live in or around Leeds and 74% were reported as living 'nearby'. Around half (47%) of the maternal grandmothers lived within ten minutes of their daughters and their families. Seventy percent of those whose mothers were still alive saw their own mother at least once a week and about a quarter (23%) saw their mother every day.

Many of the maternal grandmothers were themselves young; in more than half of cases the maternal grandmother was under retirement age. However, not all of these had paid employment; 37% of the maternal grandmothers were in paid work, with 17% working fulltime.

Hence, many of the mothers in the sample potentially had help available from their own mother during episodes of childhood illness. Indeed, around three quarters of the mothers whose own mother was still alive said that they would ask 'Grandma' for help at such times (74%) and a further 7% said that they would ask for help under certain conditions, for example if the illness was severe. It has already been noted that three quarters of the grandmothers lived nearby. Hence, mothers' reports suggest that if Grandma was potentially available to help – that is, she was still alive and living nearby – then the chances were that she would be called upon to provide help.

Clearly, although many mothers said that they would ask their own mothers for assistance during illness episodes, in the event not all of them did so. Further, grandmothers were not simply called upon to provide substitute child care, but a range of supportive tasks and emotional support. The following accounts demonstrate that the roles adopted by grandmothers during illness episodes were many and varied.

> It is nice to know that there is someone there like my mum – just to be with you. So you know that there is someone feeling as you do. Not just taking over and that.

> She would be over like a shot. She knows just what to do.

> Usually I ask her about things – advice. She will come over if I need her.

I wouldn't normally bother her, but she would help by taking them backwards and forwards to school.

I suppose pinpointing what is wrong is the main problem. If I am not sure I pop across and bring my mum over and see if she can tell.

I just phone and she is round in ten minutes.

In the following account a mother who had moved away from her family bemoans the absence of support from her own mother. Indeed, the lack of this family support was drawing the mother back to her home town.

I think worry is the main thing. [child] had meningitis when he was 8 months, so I tend to worry if he has a temperature. When we lived at [home town] I could talk to my mum. Someone with experience. That is why I want to move back ... I have no-one to turn to here.

The fact that some grandmothers lived far away often, but not always, meant that they were unable to provide support of a practical nature. However, even if grandmothers were close at hand it was often difficult for mothers to seek their help. This was for several reasons; sometimes grandmothers were unwilling to provide support. They either did not want to take the responsibility of caring for an ill child or did not think it was their place to do so.

A few times my mum would have them if they were a bit poorly, but chickenpox or measles – I have to be there. My mum gets worried and won't have them. It is too much for her. She thinks their mother should look after them. It is my problem.

I have felt put out with my mum when she has flatly refused to come in and sit with him [child].

She doesn't work. She could come over and stay but she wouldn't do that.

She would help if I am poorly – she is here in a flash, but if it was for me to go to work she thinks it is my responsibility to look after the children when they are ill. She didn't work so I don't think she thinks that I should.

While half of the grandmothers were under 60 the remaining grandparents were older. Although an account above refers to an 'agile' 69-year-old, elderly grandmothers were occasionally frail or at least considered too weak to cope with boisterous seven-year-olds.

She is 84 and has no patience. She can't look after herself.

She would be able to look after them, but she is nearly 80. If she [child] is up and about [she] would run rings around her.

While some younger grandmothers were willing to help, their own work commitments might prevent them from doing so. At the same time, mothers frequently mentioned that although Grandma was available and willing to provide help they preferred not to ask for it. Caring for their own ill child was perceived by some as their own responsibility and failing in this responsibility might lead to feelings of guilt and obligation.

She doesn't mind whether the child is ill or not – she would look after him. [but] it would depend on the day of the week if my mum was working.

I always bear in mind that it is a lot for her to cope with ... I don't like to ask too much of her.

Any help that I needed her to provide, she would do whatever she could. But I don't like to put on her and would prefer either me or his dad to do the caring.

Really, if I know she is going to be ill my parents will help out but basically I see it as my responsibility.

Occasionally caring for grandchildren could become a burden for those grandparents with several families demanding their time.

It tends to be more my dad because my mum helps my sister more with her children. They split themselves in two.

She also has my sister's children to look after as well. It is all extra to sort out.

Overall, many mothers saw their own mother as an ideal substitute carer. In more than half of the cases where the maternal grandmother was alive she would be the first person the mothers said they would rely upon to help. In 16% of the whole sample the paternal grandmother would be the most preferred helper. Thus, in all, in 58% of the sample grandparents would be the first to be approached to provide help. In the remaining cases, other female relatives (18), occasionally male relatives (4) or friends and neighbours would be asked for support during children's illness episodes. Whilst support or potential support from other relatives, friends and neighbours was important for a substantial number of mothers, for most the child's grandparents were first choice to provide substitute child care or other support.

I wouldn't like to leave him with a stranger if he was ill. If you have grandparents to help what more could you ask for?

PARTNERS AS CARERS

While members of the extended family may be perceived as 'next best' after care by the mother herself, what of the child's father? Was there any evidence that if a partner was in residence he shared the care of the sick child or at least provided the necessary degree of 'back-up' to enable both partners to make the best possible arrangements in terms of their home and work commitments?

During the initial stages of the research when the questionnaires were being developed and piloted, many of the questions relating to family networks were based on what proved to be a flawed assumption. This assumption was that if relatives were 'nearby' they provided a network of informal carers or a 'resource' that mothers could tap during illness episodes. The preceding section shows that the proximity of relatives only revealed part of the picture: such information told us only about potential rather than actual carers. This 'network' information alone revealed nothing about the extent or types of support provided by relatives.

Similarly, at the outset we assumed that the presence of a partner would be a further 'resource' for mothers to draw upon during children's illness episodes. Again, this

assumption was flawed – the presence of a partner in itself
was not indicative of any support for the mother. Indeed, as
the lone mother in the following account demonstrates, in
some cases the presence of a partner was seen as a drain on,
rather than an addition to, the family's resources.

> You hear about some of these women with children *and* a
> husband to look after. I don't know how they manage.
> We've just got ourselves to think about.

What evidence did we find of the nature and extent of the
contribution that partners (usually the children's fathers) made
to child health care?

Most of the mothers in the sample did have a partner living
with them. At the time of the final interviews 82% of the
mothers were living with a partner. To anticipate a topic treated
in more detail in later chapters, it was clear that partners were
unlikely to take time off work to care for a sick child. Chapter
7 shows that if a parent did take time off – and this in itself
was fairly unusual as mothers generally arranged alternative
care or rearranged their work – then it was likely to be the
mother. Chapter 6 demonstrates that fathers were unlikely to
go with a child to the doctor's.

Nevertheless, as we were interested in mothers' perceptions
of the division of tasks during children's illness episodes, at
the final interview we asked them about the way that child
care was shared. Over a third of the mothers claimed that child
care was shared equally with partners during illness episodes.
All but one of the rest said that they, rather than the child's
father, tended to provide most of the care. Few mothers
expressed dissatisfaction with the sharing arrangement they
had with their partner: only 19% of those mothers who
provided most of the care expressed reservations about this
and very few expressed frank dissatisfaction with their lot (7%).

Many mothers justified their satisfaction with the help their
partner provided by referring to the fact that their partners'
work demands were perceived as greater. Under these circumstances many mothers considered that it was more appropriate
for them to provide most of the care.

> He helps a lot. I do most but he helps a lot. Because he is
> on nights he sleeps through the day, so I am here then.

It has got to be me because my husband works away. That is why I am fortunate to have a good family that helps. That is part of being married to someone who has a job like this.

He is a lorry driver and is often away. I have no choice.

Mothers were aware of the possible economic implications of their partner taking a greater share of the child care burden. All of the fathers who were in employment worked fulltime and few mothers earned as much as or more than their partners. In the face of these economic implications mothers were stoical about the fact that they took on the greater part of the child care. Some of the mothers referred to their partner as the 'breadwinner', despite the fact that they also contributed to the family income.

He is there when I need him but it is me that is off work. He is the breadwinner. We can't afford for him to have time off. We can't afford for me to have time off – but it would be less. ... sometimes I get down with it if I have a lot to do, but it is one of those things about being a mother you just have to get round. Sometimes he doesn't help as much as I want him to – but if he is losing his wage we have nothing to support ourselves with.

I suppose his job is more important than mine. He earns more money so it is bound to be.

It usually doesn't come up, but if [child] were ill for any length of time it would have to be me. I suppose at the end of the day if anybody was going to lose their job it would have to be me. I can't do a lot about it.

I think it is just that he is the breadwinner. That is it. It is just the norm of things.

He is the breadwinner. We depend on his income.

Some mothers perceived that caring for their child during illness was part of their maternal role. In contrast the role of fathers was, as some of the accounts above demonstrate, often perceived as providing material comfort, in the form of a wage cheque, rather than physical care for the sick child. Mothers who were at home often emphasized that caring for their child was their 'job'.

Because I think it is my job to be here for them, that is what a mother's job is. It is my responsibility.

It is just your natural instincts. It falls on you to look after them. Children usually want you when they are not well. Sometimes I would like their dad to do more.

I am here. I am at home. They are my children and my responsibility.

[mother works part-time] He works fulltime. One has to work and one has to look after them.

That is what I am here for. Children first, work second.

That is what mums are for.

Many mothers justified the fact that they spent more time than the child's father caring for their child during illness by saying that the child would prefer to be with them. Further, some fathers were considered deficient in the skills, knowledge and attitudes necessary to care for a sick child.

About 60–70% of the time it is me. But he is good and shares the rest. Because I am sure that you know when kids are ill they scream for their mums. It is just more expedient for me to be there. It is rare we disagree.

He doesn't know what to do. He would panic. They usually come to me anyway. They are more used to me.

He hasn't much patience, so they do tend to want me when they are poorly and not their dad.

Because we have learnt with our kids that when they are poorly they want to be with their mum and not their dad. He is 100% as a father though.

When kids are ill they want their mums. There is no other way about it. As long as you have an employer that is all right, well it is fine.

I have more of an idea anyway about what the illness is and how to cope. He wouldn't have much idea.

I like to be with him when he is poorly. I don't think men are as sympathetic as women.

While the majority of mothers claimed that they felt satisfied with the sharing of care with their partner, a few mothers expressed dissatisfaction with the level of help their partner provided. Dissatisfaction was more likely if the mother was in paid work. Very few mothers said that the issue of sharing care led to disagreement but they nevertheless felt resentful that the burden of providing care, taking time off work or arranging alternative care fell generally to them.

[child] had an accident during the half term, that meant I had to be up night and day because I was working. We had a full scale battle over who had to take [child] down to the hospital. (mother working nights)

I couldn't believe it, I was starting fulltime the next day and there was no cover. I couldn't believe that she had started [being ill] that night. I had no patience. Well, her dad was moaning saying that I wasn't very sympathetic. But I said, it is all right for you. You just go off to work and it is me that is left wondering what on earth to do.

It depends on how much you make him [partner] do. He would leave it up to me if I didn't make him. He would never get up in the night. He leaves that to me. That is how it is. I wish he would take more time.

Even where there was no particular disagreement and low expectations of partners, a few mothers expressed dissatisfaction about the fact that it was *assumed* they would provide care despite the fact that they also had work commitments.

He is not prepared to take time off. One part of me thinks that that is the way it should be. But on the other hand I am fairly unsatisfied that it is always my problem. He goes off to work totally oblivious to how I have to cope. It is the system that is wrong.

He just assumes that I will see to him. I do all that . . . I get up through the night. He cares about him but I do all that.

It does get you down sometimes having them all the time when they are ill. It might be better if men had the burden sometimes.

I'm not really satisfied, no. If I can't get the time off [work]
he is just as good – but I am the one that tends to stay
at home.

Even mothers that were not in paid work sometimes felt
resentful about the fact that they bore by far the heavier burden
of providing care during children's illness episodes. The following accounts were taken from interviews with mothers who
were at home.

I suppose I can cope with it – with the first baby he helped
out, but I do it all now.

Well, usually they are ill during the day and he is at work.
If it is at night he has to go to work the next day so I get
up at night with them. It is tiring. I do understand that he
has to get up for work. But then again I have to cope all
day with them being ill.

It is always the woman that does it. It shouldn't always be
the wife. It does get you down sometimes having them all
the time when they are ill.

He just doesn't do it. They are his kids as well so he should
take his share of the responsibility.

The third of mothers who claimed that their partners took
an equal share of child care during children's illness episodes
tended to explain this arrangement in terms of their own work
commitments or the lack of flexibility of their work compared
with their partner's work. Many mothers mentioned the fact
that children were the responsibility of both parents; sometimes this was irrespective of their relative work commitments.

He does as much as I do. Because of work, so that I can
continue to work.

Because of him being self-employed it is easier for him. My
employers are very unsympathetic towards you being off
for that . . . If I had the choice there would be times I'd rather
be at home myself.

We can't have it any other way [than shared], it is like a
shift system – it works for us. I just think it is right to share
instead of putting it all on one person.

If he is at home he does his share. It gives me a rest. I used to do it all ... it used to get me down doing everything.

A child is both parents' responsibility and I think you should work at it together.

With working, if they were ill now, one of us, whoever it suited most at the time, would take time off. Because like everything else, I think you should share.

It was unclear from mothers' accounts what 'taking an equal share' actually meant. There was little evidence that fathers took an 'equal share' in carrying out many of the caring tasks necessary during illness episodes. Taking the child to the doctor's and providing care during school absence, particularly if this involved taking time off work, were predominantly carried out by the mother or by other female relatives. When mothers claimed that their partners took an equal share they may have meant that their partners did 'help' or provided support of an emotional rather than a practical nature. It may also have been the case that the term 'equal' was used in the Orwellian sense – some shares counting as 'more equal' than others. What may have counted as equal for women and their partners may have been quite different. The way in which care provided by men was measured by mothers was within the context of low expectations, or as one mother put it:

He is ever so good – for a fella.

RELATIVES AND PARTNERS – MOTHERS' 'TREASURES'?

Interviews following up illness episodes during the monitoring stage of the study indicated that relatives were frequently involved in providing substitute child care either as primary or secondary carers. Clearly, many mothers, whether they were in work or not, did rely on relatives to provide help and support when their children were ill. At the final interview mothers were asked to review the help they had received during illness episodes over the preceding year. Sixty-five percent of the mothers claimed that relatives (not including partners) had provided some form of help on at least one occasion. This figure is larger than the number of mothers who we found to be dependent on relatives to provide care during the monitoring stage. This could be explained by the fact that mothers were only asked about the care of the sick child and relatives may well have provided alternative forms of support. Grandparents and other relatives could be enlisted to collect prescriptions, fetch shopping, deliver siblings to school or provide mothers with moral support or advice.

About a third of the sample said that they had had no help from relatives in connection with their child's illness episodes during the previous year. The number of mothers with relatives living nearby was greater than the number who in fact received help; this may indicate that potential support and actual support are indeed different. The fact that mothers had not received help can be explained in a variety of ways. The most simple explanation is that mothers did not perceive that they needed any help and therefore did not seek any. Their children may have had either very trivial and/or shortlived illness which did not unduly upset the family's normal routine. A second reason may have been the absence of local kin. The lack of family living nearby did not, however, preclude the possibility of relatives providing help. Some mothers mentioned that grandparents would come to stay if children suffered from more lengthy illness episodes. The following account demonstrates that even non-local kin could be called upon in emergencies.

The only thing that would make it easier would be if my mum lived around the corner. [but] If it was major she [child] would go to my mother's or my mother would come here.

A third reason which would explain the lack of help from some local kin was the fact that relatives may have been physically frail and therefore either unable to provide some forms of help or mothers would be reluctant to seek their support because of their frail condition. Fourth, relatives living nearby may have been unavailable either because they were themselves in paid work or had other family commitments which prevented them from providing support. Last, although relatives may have been able and 'available' to provide assistance they may have been unwilling to do so or mothers may have been unwilling to seek their support – this may have occurred for a variety of reasons.

Hence, as a number of authors have pointed out before, using relatives to provide substitute child care, although preferred by most mothers, is not without its attendant problems. Relatives may be unavailable, unwilling or unable to provide support and the help they do provide may not add up to a comprehensive package of support for mothers caring for a sick child.

Calling upon relatives, and in particular grandmothers, for help may not always therefore present the ideal solution to child care problems which emerge as a result of children's illness. Relatives, particularly close female ones, may be the most trusted, reliable and accessible helpers from the point of view of the mother and the most preferred carers from the point of view of the child. The help they provide may often be cheap or 'free'. But such help is not the answer to every mother's child care difficulties. First, relatives may not be available to provide care and even if they are they may not be willing to step in at short notice with small remuneration. Relatives may be in paid work themselves or live far away and therefore have other commitments to juggle. In our sample, of the maternal grandmothers living nearby, 37% were in paid work. Despite this, many mothers did depend on help from grandparents and in particular the maternal grandmother.

On the question of payment, some mothers recognized that paying for help was not a simple matter; they were often in low paid work and therefore would be unable to pay 'market' rates for child care. At the same time, some carers were apparently unwilling to accept cash payment for their help. Some mothers felt that it was inappropriate to offer cash as the ties of kinship altered the relationship between themselves and the carers or, as Abrams *et al.* (1989) put it:

> Informal care . . . is rooted not in commitment to tasks but in attachment to persons; it is a property of relationships not jobs. Even when the relationships within which informal care is given are founded upon implicit or explicit contracts, it is personal relationships that get these contracts enforced.

However, the fact that mothers felt under obligation was an indication that they felt that the 'contractual' relationship with carers was less than reciprocal and possibly exploitative, at least in the short term.

The issue of the gender of carers is also important. It is clear that most tasks associated with child health care were carried out by women, mostly by the child's mother, and that most help was provided by other female relatives or friends. In our sample, as in the study by Abrams *et al.*, 'Between mothers and daughters in particular, almost any call for help [was] normally considered to be legitimate'. Children's fathers did step in to provide care in some cases, very occasionally fathers took time off work to care for their sick child, but as this and subsequent chapters demonstrate the contribution of fathers, male relatives and other men to child health care in the home was limited. Caring, giving care, denotes both feelings and service. As most caring roles are performed by women, according to Finch and Groves (1983), caring is central to definitions of femininity.

Within the economy, 'caring' work is generally of low status and is mainly performed by women on low wages. Within the domestic economy the costs of caring – either for elderly relatives, spouses or children in sickness and health – are conveniently ignored by policy makers as they are carried out within the 'private' realm of the home and within the context of close personal relationships. The fact that, within our sample, the preponderance of care was provided by mothers and female relatives suggests implications for working women and for their relationships with their female kin and friends. Mothers in paid work frequently depended on other women in order for them to be able to meet their work commitments. In some cases, elderly, sometimes ailing relatives were subsidizing maternal employment by providing low or no cost child care during illness episodes. As Finch and Groves suggest, 'Unlike the labour contracts negotiated through the cash nexus, caring is a work role whose form and content is shaped (and constantly reshaped) by our intimate social and sexual relationships'. At a general level, even where female relatives are willing and able to provide care, the situation remains problematic. Those without relatives have to make alternative arrangements, again frequently dependent on women working for no or low wages providing child care and nursing services.

Although one mother talked of 'colossal arguments' with her male partner over the issue of providing child care during sickness episodes, most mothers had little expectation of help and thereby avoided disagreement about the fact that only a little help from partners was forthcoming. Mothers, whether in paid work or not, largely accepted a 'traditional' division of labour with regards to caring tasks during illness. Indeed, providing care during illness was often perceived as being a role particularly appropriate for the child's mother. In general fathers were not expected to provide care during illness, especially if this implied any disruption to their work. If mothers could not provide care themselves, the most likely substitute carer was not the child's father but a female relative. In the end, the responsibility for providing or arranging alternative care mainly fell to mothers.

The burden of responsibility was often heaviest for those mothers in paid work. Many mothers perceived that whether fathers worked or not was not a matter open to choice: if work was available men were expected to work, while for women there was perceived to be more of a choice. However, at the same time many mothers claimed that they worked because their families 'needed the money'; the so-called 'choice' about working was in fact governed by economic imperatives. During illness episodes it was the fact that mothers but not fathers were working that seemed to be the factor that constrained decision making. It seemed that it was the mothers' but not the fathers' work that was the 'problem'. If it was a case of missing work and forgoing earnings or holidays, it was the mother who was expected to take time off. We will end this chapter with an account from a mother who was attempting to perform the 'juggling act'.

> You've got to work today. I think it is always the mother that gets it and not the father. Even though you are working you still have to do all the running about to the doctor's and hospital. I am very lucky, I have got my mum, without her I would find it a lot more difficult. There should be something better.

6

Women's employment and health service use

In addition to the practical decisions concerning the provision of care for the sick child and the decisions bound up in deciding whether or not a child should attend school, mothers and sometimes other carers (including school staff) are obliged to make decisions about the sort of care the sick child needs to treat the disease and to alleviate distressing symptoms. The main thrust of preceding chapters has been the way in which disease impinges on normal daily life and the strategies mothers and other carers use in order to manage any changes in routine. An area touched upon in Chapter 4 was the way in which the illness 'state' was negotiated by the child, its mother, other family members and school staff. However, others outside the immediate family and social network may be involved in the negotiation of the sick role. Health professionals such as the child's GP, health visitor, practice nurse, GP's receptionist and chemist may be involved at various stages during illness episodes and may all contribute to the decision making process.

The aim of this chapter is to focus more directly on the child's 'illness' in order to examine the ways in which decisions concerning the physical care of the child are made. The questions raised in this chapter include how mothers make preliminary diagnoses of illness – how do they know when their child is 'poorly'? Under what sort of circumstances would the help of professionals be sought? What sort of home nursing strategies do mothers and other carers adopt to reduce the child's distress during illness episodes? How do mothers 'treat' disease, with or in the absence of advice from health professionals? How dependent is this treatment on the use of proprietary drugs? Last, how do mothers rate the help they receive from outside sources?

Throughout the chapter some common themes are addressed, chiefly whether mothers in paid work and those at home behave differently or have different attitudes in relation to health care issues. It might be the case that working mothers use health professionals in different ways; they might seek medical attention early in order to 'nip' developing conditions 'in the bud' or they might not seek the advice of their GP at all, as appointment systems are not designed with the working mother in mind and surgeries might be at 'awkward' times.

Clearly, many of the issues addressed are common to all childhood illness episodes irrespective of maternal employment and as Mayall (1986) pointed out:

> Most of mothers' health work for their children takes place at home, out of the public gaze, and much of it is the humdrum stuff of everyday life . . . When children are ill, most of the care and treatment is given by mothers at home and only the tip of the illness iceberg is seen by outsiders.

The aim of this chapter is to examine more closely this 'humdrum stuff of everyday life' by presenting and discussing mothers' accounts of their children's illness episodes from the moment when their child started to show signs of ill health to the time when the child fully regained her/his normal state of health. The chapter will begin with a brief description of the types of conditions which led to school absence over the monitoring period and will go on to describe the ways in which mothers decided their child was ill and their subsequent actions to treat the disease and relieve its symptoms.

SICKNESS AND SCHOOL ABSENCE

The most common cause of school absence recorded during the monitoring stage of the research was an upper respiratory tract infection. If coughs and colds and ear and throat infections are counted together, these would account for almost half of the school absence due to illness (134/282). There were a further 60 episodes of gastrointestinal conditions, six rash conditions and 66 'other' conditions: these ranged from boils to bangs on the head. Mothers were also interviewed following their children's hospital outpatient appointments or hospitalization.

The incidence of disease was not evenly distributed over the monitoring period: there was a definite peak in the number of illness episodes in November/December and a smaller peak in February. The November peak coincided with the 'flu epidemic of autumn 1989. The incidence of the various types of illness all seemed to peak at around the same times of year.

In general, illness episodes were short; absence data from the schools revealed that more than half of the children with gastrointestinal conditions were off school for one day or less while for 31% of the cough episodes, children were off for a day or less. Two thirds of all episodes resulted in two days or less away from school. (It is important to remember, however, that duration of absence may not have been the same as the duration of the disease.)

THE FIRST SIGNS OF ILLNESS

As far as can be ascertained from our data, the ways in which a mother decided that her child was ill and the diagnosis of the condition were not affected by whether or not she was in paid work.

Deciding when and whether a child was 'ill' was not always easy. Chapter 4 described in some detail the ways in which 'illness' was negotiated and the apparent elasticity of the term.

It was clear from many accounts describing the onset of illness that mothers felt that they had special knowledge about their child and about their child's appearance and general behaviour which made them particularly receptive to any changes which might signify the onset of illness. At the interviews following illness episodes, mothers were asked to describe what first made them think that their child was not well. The most frequently mentioned first sign of illness was a clinical symptom; this was mentioned in half of the episodes (50%). Showing signs of having a temperature was a clear indicator of illness for many mothers; however loss of appetite, pallor, lethargy and changes in sleep patterns were also frequently mentioned. (Temperatures were not usually recorded by a thermometer; mothers were sensitive to other signs of a raised temperature.) Children's own reports of feelings of nausea or complaints of aches or pains were also mentioned as initial indicators of illness. Frequently the first sign occurred during the night.

> She came to me and she was right hot. She had a temperature during the night. She complained of her throat hurting.

> He just looked really pale and didn't want to eat. He was sleeping a lot.

> She was crying. She woke me up – she had been sick in the bed.

In some cases a change in behaviour marked the beginning of illness or was seen as a sign which preceded the onset of illness. These behavioural changes were sometimes peculiar to a child and the mother depended on her store of special knowledge or intuition about her child to interpret these changes as a sign of impending illness. Similarly, general changes in appearance also signified changes in health; sometimes these signs were peculiar to a child while others would have been instantly recognized by any mother as a sign of imminent illness. Many of the mothers used a special vocabulary when describing illness, using terms such as 'nattery', 'lolly' and 'wittery' which specifically referred to children's illness behaviours and were sure signs that their child was 'under the weather'. In the following account, a mother used a range of terms which conjure up the particularly awkward and uncooperative behaviour her child adopted during illness episodes.

> She had just started to get niggly, cranky and fidgety. Whereas usually they will play with each other – Sunday the niggles started.

In the accounts below, mothers drew on their special knowledge of their child and their experience of previous illness behaviours to justify their fears that their child was becoming unwell.

It is a silly thing to say – she always eats before she is going to be poorly. She ate really well. I said to [her dad] that she was going to be poorly. It is as if her body is telling her to eat now because she is going to be off it. And she gets upset about comments and is, well, not exactly naughty, but easily upset.

His eyes were bloodshot. You can usually tell with his eyes.

Just him lying about and being quiet, which isn't him at all.

Last Saturday morning she didn't want to get up out of bed, normally she is up at the crack of dawn. She was weepy and I didn't seem to be able to get her to move.

Some conditions did not 'count' as illnesses, while in other cases symptoms had been going on for some time and there was no clear onset. For example, sometimes it was not clear when a condition changed from being 'just a cold' to an 'illness' or at least to a condition that demanded some attention. Frequently, the first mentioned sign that the child was becoming ill was the fact that the child had been sent home from school 'sick'. In the case of coughs and colds, this may not have been the very first indication of illness, but it was at this stage that the condition became noteworthy – if school staff noticed something and made the effort to point it out in a very deliberate way, it meant that something 'had to be done'. This even applied if the mother herself considered that there was little ailing her child.

I thought it was just a normal cold ... he didn't want to do anything and he looked pasty. Then one of the teachers thought he was coming down with something.

She was dizzy at school – I think it was the heat of the hall. The headmistress brought her home. She was all right in the morning and she was all right when she came home. (the child had a cough)

Well, she went to school and the teacher told her not to come back in because she wasn't well. I wouldn't have sent her the next day anyway. She wasn't well.

Sometimes predispositions to certain conditions or recurrent episodes of disease alerted mothers to the onset of symptoms.

Mothers had particular worries if a child was seen as especially vulnerable or susceptible to disease and these concerns often prompted action in the face of fairly minor symptoms. Other family members suffering from a particular condition might also prompt a mother to look for the first signs of similar illness appearing in her child.

> Well, we all had runny noses. He always gets a cough when he gets any sort of chill. He had whooping cough at two – it is a recurrence of that. He had a cough and it built up worse and worse over the two weeks.

Chapter 4 describes in some detail how children were sometimes suspected of feigning or exaggerating symptoms of illness. The onset of feigned symptoms was often perceived to coincide with particular events at home or unpleasant school lessons or bullying. Sometimes 'non-specific' symptoms were seen as 'psychological' or a sign that the child was worrying about something.

> I thought she was shamming in the morning . . . [but] the school contacted me.

> He tends to worry. He had been bullied up at school. I think it has run him down. He tells us when it is too late.

> She was tired in the morning, but she doesn't like Wednesdays. So I thought I had best send her then she didn't think that I was going to let her have Wednesdays off.

Sometimes initial symptoms were disregarded as they seemed trivial, but subsequent developments prompted alarm and action. In the following account a mother describes this progression from mild interest and concern to a sense of panic.

> It started swelling. It wasn't obvious . . . his jaws started swelling at first . . . but when it went under his eyes I started to panic. It looked horrendous then.

Occasionally mothers could not identify specific signs or symptoms of illness, but just trusted their intuitive judgement that their child was 'sickening' for an illness.

> She was off colour on the Sunday. A bit lolly. Not quite right.

He is run down. He doesn't like to go to bed and he can't switch off.

He looked grey. He wasn't right at all. He wasn't off colour, he was just tired. He just didn't want attention.

Mothers often used a range of indicators of impending illness and, as some of the accounts above demonstrate, the process of decision making was dynamic. Further, the process was very individualized; changes in the child's appearance or behaviour would be measured against a standard of what was perceived as 'normal' for that child. While some children became excited and attention seeking during the onset of illness, others became lethargic. Deciding whether a child was ill or not was sometimes instantaneous: if a child got up in the night vomiting they were deemed ill. With other symptoms the process was sometimes drawn out over days or weeks and sometimes illness did not 'materialize' despite the mother perceiving 'warning signs' such as pallor or behavioural changes. Most of the mothers claimed that their child's 'illness' had come on suddenly. However, the distinction between the onset of symptoms and the child actually becoming 'ill' was not always clear. For example, a child might have had a cough for 14 days but it might be claimed that she had only been 'ill' for two days, the onset of 'illness' coinciding with the child complaining of earache or some other more worrying symptom. In 75% of episodes the child was said to have become 'ill' suddenly. The fact that illness was seen as something that struck suddenly and with little warning is obviously an important issue. Illness episodes required rapid decision making. Many decisions arose either in the middle of the night or early in the morning. One mother described her feelings when her child awoke in the night vomiting.

I wasn't worried about the illness, she was just sick. My main worry was the fact that I would have to go to work and what would I do . . . I was having nightmares all night . . . Just all the hassle . . . Well, her dad was moaning saying I wasn't very sympathetic but I said, it is all right for you, you just go off to work, it is me left wondering what on earth to do.

Decisions concerning the treatment of the disease and more practical arrangements concerning the care of the child were often made at particularly stressful times: either after the mother had been woken from sleep or first thing in the morning when the mother and other family members were preparing for work, school and the demands of a 'normal' day.

CAUSES OF DISEASE AND CAUSES OF ILLNESS

Chapter 4 describes some of the causes of illness identified by mothers and demonstrates that schools were seen as a particular source of illness. Various 'lay theories of illness causation' have been discussed elsewhere (Ley, 1988; Helman, 1990); four different sources of ill health have been identified. The first of these is found within the ill person themselves; the second, in the natural world; the third, in the social world; and the last, in the supernatural world. Mothers' accounts which ascribed a cause for the child developing an illness, or a reason for a child becoming ill at any given time, can be loosely fitted into one but more frequently into several of the above categories, although the supernatural world was least likely to be identified as a cause of illness.

First, some children were seen as being prone to illness or more vulnerable to particular conditions, for example, coughs or 'bad chests'. Birth trauma or severe illness during infancy were identified as factors which could 'weaken' a child and make her more susceptible to certain conditions. The following account demonstrates how a mother made a causal link between her child's early life and later illnesses. It is unclear, however, whether the mother thought that the child being given oxygen was the cause of later 'weakness' or whether it was the condition which had led to this intervention which had caused the coughs in later life. Further, being 'prone' to a particular condition tended to mean that the stimulus of a change in the weather was needed before the child suffered any ill effects.

He were given oxygen when he was first born. He gets that cough every year as the weather turns colder.

In 12 episodes the cause of illness was perceived to be the result of a particular weakness or precondition in the child.

Frequently, the child or its parent was perceived as somehow responsible for the development of a condition because they did not take measures to prevent its onset. Behaving in certain careful or careless ways might prevent or cause ill health. For example, a mother thought her child's condition resulted from the fact that she had 'had a bath with the window open'. However, it is unclear whether children of the age of the study sample (6–7) were thought to be responsible themselves for their own ill health or whether this was the responsibility of their parents.

Sometimes the child's personality was identified as a source of illness. Some children were 'worriers' and this led to physical symptoms. One child suffered from vomiting and this, according to his mother, was the result of excitement.

He is poorly after every birthday. I was expecting him up in the night – the excitement – I knew what it was, just birthday excitement.

The natural world was frequently identified as a cause or source of ill health. A change in the weather or severe weather conditions were specifically mentioned in 14 episodes as a cause of illness. Sometimes, as accounts from Chapter 4 demonstrated, the threat from the natural world was exacerbated by interventions or lack of them from the social world; for example, children were 'thrown out' of school without coats in wet weather. A change in the weather and a lack of adequate precautions in the light of this change were seen as a cause of ill health which resulted in coughs and colds, earache and sore throats.

Only the weather getting colder. We hadn't bothered about a hat before.

I think it is just the time of year. The change in weather.

Well, it was windy, that is what starts it.

Whether the weather, the social world or lack of personal responsibility are causes of disease has been questioned. Isaacs (1987) comments:

When the various myths surrounding colds have been subject to scientific scrutiny the evidence has been that catching chills, getting cold feet, exposure to draughts and so on have no effect on susceptibility to colds.

It seems from such comments that lay models of illness causation are definitely the poor relations of 'scientific' explanations of ill health; if such models are not treated as frankly mistaken they are certainly perceived as being inferior. However, becoming ill is a negotiable process which may well be affected by the social world, psychological factors and possibly the weather. Although scientific evidence has not proven that such factors cause 'colds', that is, a particular type of disease, it is unlikely that evidence of this type could prove that these factors do not cause 'illness' as they may affect the way that individuals negotiate the sick role and therefore whether or not they 'succumb' to the disease.

A further source of illness from the natural world identified in mothers' accounts was food. Sometimes food 'caused' illness because certain kinds of food were perceived to lead to certain types of disorder. For example, in the following account, 'cold' food was thought to 'chill' the stomach.

She had an ice lolly and I think that could have chilled her stomach – the ice lolly or the baths.

Food additives were seen as a potential source of illness, although sometimes it was not clear whether the source of illness was contaminated foodstuffs or whether some children were perceived to be sensitive to some foods or additives.

I wondered whether it was a different Pepsi-cola. When she has one type of cola she ends up coughing and wheezing later.

She had been to her friend's for her tea so I thought it was something she ate.

Eating too much or overindulgence in particular types of food were also perceived as a cause of illness. Again it is unclear whether children were held responsible for their behaviour.

He went to a party and I think he had a lot to eat – sweet stuff.

Overeating before she went to bed.

Too much food. It was her brother's birthday party.

The social world was perceived as a major 'cause' of illness. Even though colds, bugs and viruses were 'going around', it was often perceived that they were 'caught' or 'picked up' at school or other children 'passed them on'. The monitoring took place during the winter of 1989 which coincided with an influenza epidemic. Although children were therefore at risk from the 'natural world', they were perceived to be at particular risk playing with their friends or being in contact with other children in school or at home.

All the kids at school had it.

Well, I think there are a lot of colds down at school.

They said there was a virus going around school.

She caught it from her sister.

In 14% of episodes children were thought to have 'caught' or 'picked up' an illness that was 'going around'. It is interesting in the accounts describing food as a cause of illness that children seemed more likely to suffer ill effects from food they had received at a friend's house rather than at home – as though food outside home is more likely to be contaminated. The swimming baths were also identified as a place where children 'picked up' chills or 'tummy upsets'.

The children who feigned illness were perceived as reacting to pressures of the social world; feigning was regarded as a deliberate ploy to stay at home in order to get 'pampered' or to avoid bullying or specific events at school such as school trips or PE lessons.

The sources and causes of illness identified by mothers were many and varied – a new brand of washing powder was thought to lead to an itchy rash condition, the cat's flea powder was perceived to cause a bad cough. Occasionally mothers were very specific about the cause of ill health and were clear about how the situation could be alleviated.

The state of this house. It is a safety hazard. There are gaps in their window frames – draughts. We have got to be rehoused. When they [the council] will get round to it I don't know. I don't want them a winter in that room.

It seems from mothers' accounts that some conditions were regarded as avoidable by taking certain precautions. Yet, while mothers recognized that they could take various measures to guard their child's health, the child faced many external threats and illness was an inevitable, unpredictable and – for many children – frequent occurrence.

SEEKING MEDICAL ADVICE

One of the aims of the research was to investigate whether certain groups used health services in different ways. For example, was it the case that mothers who were at home were more likely to seek the advice of their GP because they were able to attend daytime surgeries? Did mothers who worked fulltime tend to delay seeking medical attention for their children because surgeries were at 'inconvenient' times? Or were behaviours across the groups the opposite to those described above? Could it be that mothers who were at home were in a position to 'wait and see'? That is, if children showed minor symptoms they might be prepared to delay consultation or not consult at all. In contrast, mothers in work might rush to their doctor at the first sign of illness to 'nip in the bud' any developing condition in order to avoid school absence for their child and work absence for themselves. Or, could it be that working mothers were more likely to demand appointments at specific times or to seek advice from the chemist to avoid time consuming visits to their GP?

We were also interested in the perception of the delivery of health services across different groups; for example, did working mothers feel that they had difficulty getting access to their GP at convenient times or did mothers without certain resources, such as a telephone, find access more difficult? Or was it the case that maternal employment made no difference to consultation rates or to the level of satisfaction with health services? If so, what factors did influence, for example, whether or not a child consulted the doctor?

The decision to seek medical advice, like the decision to keep the child away from school, was not taken lightly. Further, the decision was frequently negotiated between the mother, child, other family members and school staff. Nevertheless, the chief responsibility for the decision to consult a GP mainly lay with the child's mother and it was mainly she that attended with the child. Occasionally fathers accompanied their children to the doctor's, but this was a rare occurrence.

The decision to consult

Previous research on doctor consultation in cases of respiratory infection has established that, irrespective of social class, the main factor which determines how a mother manages an illness episode and whether or not the child consults a GP is the severity of that particular episode (Wyke *et al.*, 1990). The same study found lower consultation rates amongst children of working mothers, but contradictory findings were obtained elsewhere (Clarke and Hewison, 1991). These two studies did, however, differ in terms of age of the study children, ethnicity and other sociodemographic characteristics of the sample. Further, neither examined the characteristics of maternal employment in terms of hours and other work related factors which might constrain health decision making.

During Phase II of our study, there was a fairly even split between those episodes which led to doctor consultation and those which did not. In 136 (48%) episodes the child was seen by her general practitioner. There were seven episodes when the local chemist or the practice nurse was approached for advice. In addition, several children were seen by a hospital consultant at an outpatient clinic. In 27 episodes the family doctor was consulted on more than one occasion.

For the episodes where the mother did seek medical advice, in 20% of these the doctor was called out. In 63% of such episodes the child was seen at the surgery; in 5%, mothers were given phone advice by the GP and in 6%, advice by the receptionist. In the remaining cases the child was seen by a hospital doctor.

During the monitoring stage of the research, of those children absent from school on at least one occasion, 73% consulted the doctor at least once; 22% consulted three or more times during that period. Children who were either not absent from school at all or had illnesses during holidays or weekends may also have sought medical advice at some time. Hence, we estimate that about two thirds of the children in the sample saw the doctor at least once during the course of the winter of 1989. What factors led to this large number of consultations?

Consultation and conditions

Some conditions were more likely to lead to doctor consultation than others. The reason why this occurred will be explored later but, in short, the doctor tended not to be consulted if any or all of the following factors pertained:

- if symptoms were either minor or non-distressing;
- if the mother felt confident that she could deal with the situation without advice;
- if the mother thought there was 'no treatment' for the condition;
- if the illness was very shortlived.

Not surprisingly, these factors were often dependent on the nature of the condition.

In the case of earache and sore throat it was likely that the doctor would be contacted. In episodes of this type, medical help was sought in 78% of cases. In contrast, for vomiting and diarrhoea it was far less likely that the child would see a doctor: in only 18% of episodes of 'tummy upsets' did consultation occur. With coughs and colds there was a more even division between those who did and those who did not consult, with 57% seeking medical advice. In the six episodes of rash conditions, all children consulted while for general conditions, again the division was almost even with a 52% consultation rate.

Severity and consultation

Deciding whether or not to seek medical advice was a fraught business for mothers. If a mother decided to seek advice when the child exhibited fairly trivial signs of ill health, she might be accused of 'wasting' the doctor's time or of being 'overprotective' whereas if she 'ignored' these signs she would face criticism and guilt if subsequently the child developed more serious symptoms. Which symptoms, though, are trivial and which serious? Can signs and symptoms be divided in this way or is it more a matter of degree? Further, is a particular type of cough more serious or is duration a more important factor in deciding whether a child with a cough should consult or not?

In the case of school attendance the assessment of disease severity, the nature of disease and the child's reaction to illness were identified as factors which might influence mothers' decision making. In the case of the decision concerning doctor consultation the nature of the disease was clearly a factor associated with consultation but so too, at least as far as coughs and colds were concerned, was the severity of the disease and this included a measure of duration.

Consulting for coughs and colds

Coughs and colds formed around a third of the episodes in the study and resulted in an almost even division of 'consulters' and 'non-consulters'. For these conditions we had some measure of illness severity.

Although coughs and colds are very common, as Hannay (1979) indicated, GPs witness only 'the tip of the illness iceberg'. In Chapter 1, figures were given from a large study in the north of England which found that about 28% of children in the 5–11 age band had suffered from a cough during the preceding month, but only a quarter of these had consulted their GP. Despite this relatively low consultation rate, respiratory illness forms a major part of the GP's caseload: in the 1981–2 National Morbidity Study, 30% of all consultations for children under 11 were for respiratory disease (Royal College of General Practitioners, 1986). Yet, many episodes of coughs and colds are self-limiting and the doctor can do very little to contribute to the child's recovery so in some cases where consultation does occur, parents could be accused of using health services inappropriately (Lau, 1987). However, a condition which is regarded as trivial by a GP may not appear so to the anxious parents of an ill and distressed child. Further, the reasons why parents seek the advice of a doctor are not always simple. If a child has a distressing viral infection a doctor may not be able to offer any treatment but this may not inhibit consultation. Doctor consultation is not simply a matter of receiving a diagnosis and collecting a 'cure'. Doctors can also offer explanations, advice on treatment and prognosis and, of course, reassurance.

As far as our sample was concerned, disease severity did seem to be an important predictor of doctor consultation for coughs and colds. The severity questionnaire used as part of the Phase II interview revealed that consulters had much higher severity scores than non-consulters. This supports the findings of previous studies using the same severity instrument (Wyke *et al.*, 1990; Clarke and Hewison, 1991). Indeed the main justification given by mothers for seeking medical advice was the nature and severity of the child's condition. Conversely, those that did not contact a GP justified this decision on the grounds that the condition was 'trivial' or not serious enough to 'bother the doctor'. In more than half of the episodes where consultation occurred, mothers justified their decision to consult in terms of the distressing or severe symptoms their child was suffering.

Because her throat was getting sore when she was swallowing.

His cough, I didn't like it when he coughed, his chest was heaving.

Because of the lack of sleep and not eating, then she started getting the temperature.

With a trapped finger – I ran it under cold water and noticed the end was loose, that was when I decided it was a hospital job. I washed it and it moved. I thought 'uuurrgghh'.

Well, because of her earache. I can deal with a cold but I can't see what is going on in her ears.

A symptom which was mentioned as being particularly worrying was a temperature and the fact that the child had this symptom was perceived as a reason to seek medical advice.

When the temperature was 102. That was it. I rang straight away.

The cough was worrying me – plus the temperature. She was burning.

I couldn't get the temperature down.

GP consultation and mothers' employment

We found that the use made of health services did not differ between mothers at home and those in paid work. The proportions of families consulting a GP were very similar (just under half) and for coughs and colds, where the most detailed severity data were available, there were no differences in the severity threshold for consulting across the groups, although within each group consulters had much higher severity scores than non-consulters.

In interpreting these findings, differences in the severity distributions need to be borne in mind: the higher proportion of very mild episodes in children whose mothers were at home might have suggested a lower rate of consultation (since severity is much the strongest predictor of consultation in this group: Wyke *et al.*, 1990), but this might have been completely offset by a higher rate of consultation amongst parents of children with more severe disorders, also over-represented in the 'at home' group.

THE DECISION TO CONSULT – OTHER FACTORS

Although the severity of a particular episode was associated with the decision to consult for coughs and colds, it became clear from mothers' accounts that severity alone did not decide the matter in all cases. For some children a previous illness or the presence of other disease could mean that fairly trivial symptoms could be perceived as very threatening.

> [diarrhoea and vomiting] I rang the doctor's as soon as it opened. I thought if there was anything I could give her to stop the vomiting. With her diabetes I had to make sure that her blood sugar didn't get too low.

> ... he had this cold and I thought if it got on his chest he might start with asthma.

> ... when he starts coughing we know that if we don't get something it will go on into an asthma attack.

In other cases the fact that a child had a recurrent condition meant that mothers were 'used to' dealing with the condition and did not therefore seek medical advice. If neighbouring children had also suffered from a similar condition mothers might seek the advice of other parents.

I think I was pretty confident that I knew what it was – knowing that other children had a similar thing. They are very busy [at the doctor's].

Well, when I spoke to the other mums about it I was told that it was going around and that it lasted about five days. I realized that it was a shortlived virus type thing so I played it by ear. If it had got worse I would have called the doctor.

Because she had the same symptoms as her sister . . . the doctor had been out to her sister earlier in the week so I knew what to do. I gave her some of her sister's medicine – Amoxyl and paracetamol.

Mothers frequently used their knowledge about their child or the medical history of other family members to justify their decision to consult. For some mothers the decision to consult was to 'nip in the bud' developing conditions or to get prescribed medication for a diagnosed condition. In both cases mothers relied on their store of experience to justify their action.

I thought, he does suffer a lot with tonsillitis – I usually leave it but I thought I might as well get something straightaway then I might catch it early. We only noticed it as he got up, he had just had it a couple of hours.

Well I found with [her brother] that that was the only way or it would drag on and on. I thought it would be better to catch it [early].

Well she couldn't stand anything in her mouth and she was refusing food. Her brother had been [to the doctor's] a few days before and he had needed antibiotics – we thought she needed likewise.

The short duration of the illness or the trivial nature of the illness sometimes delayed consultation. Sometimes an illness was severe but shortlived and in other cases the symptoms dragged on but were not perceived to be serious; in both cases mothers might decide not to consult.

It was all over so quickly. One minute she is dying, the next minute she is up.

She was all right. She was as right as a bobbin. I did think if it went on much longer ... but she was all right by morning.

If it had gone on longer I would have done. But ... she seemed OK, it was gone later that afternoon.

If his temperature had lasted more than 24 hours I would have taken him down. But doctors don't like to be fetched for a cold. I sort him out myself.

While illnesses of short duration were not worrying, those which were at first perceived as trivial could later be seen as more threatening just because of their prolonged nature. Severity then was a dynamic term, partly determined by illness duration.

The cough was getting worse instead of clearing up as it usually does after a couple of weeks. It was into the third week. He was upset with it which is why I ended up taking him to the doctor's. He got himself right miserable.

I didn't phone until I was very concerned. I had to be insistent for a visit. He couldn't walk to the toilet he was so weak. He had just started being sick and had diarrhoea. I was worried – it was the third day.

He had had a bad night. He had had it for about four weeks [cough]. It wasn't getting worse but it wasn't getting better. I was at a loss what to do.

The actual timing of the decision to consult was sometimes determined by practical considerations which did not relate to the illness or its severity but more to the organization of GP services. For example, if a child was ill on Friday a mother might seek the advice of the GP sooner rather than later as normal appointments would not be available until after the weekend.

Then I thought with Christmas coming I'd best get it before the holidays so I took him last night.

Because she was distressed and it was bad that morning. I thought I'll have to get something for over the weekend for her. She had had it a while. I had been hanging on.

The fact that the illness was becoming worse or was prolonged was mentioned as the main reason for consulting the doctor in 13% of episodes. Of those that did not consult, the main reason for not doing so was the short duration of the episode and this was mentioned in 53% of episodes.

Advice from school staff or other parents could also prompt consultation. School staff sometimes suggested diagnoses and the very fact that staff had commented upon a child's health was sufficient to confirm that a visit to the GP was necessary.

He had his medicine and it hadn't worked and his teacher was a bit worried about him, so I took him back. I knew there was something.

Everyone has been saying, 'Get him seen to, there is something wrong with that kid'.

[rash] Because the school asked. They thought it was German measles.

Sometimes mothers contacted the surgery for reassurance or to report an illness. This was particularly the case with infectious illnesses. The first of the following accounts was taken from an interview with a mother whose child had had vomiting and diarrhoea and the second chickenpox. In both cases the mothers had spoken to the GP's receptionist.

I just wanted to know if it was a bug and if I should do anything. She said she had had it herself and that it was a quick thing. I was reassured by that, so I thought I would leave it for a day and see.

Just to notify them. The receptionist said it wouldn't be necessary to see the doctor unless she was particularly ill with it.

Some mothers claimed that they had an intuitive sense of whether or not it was appropriate to call the doctor and used this intuition to justify their decision concerning consultation.

Because I didn't think it was important enough. A mother knows if it is really necessary to call a doctor.

Mothers' intuition. Well, you can get things from the chemist. I am not the type to go to the doctor's with every little thing.

Well, I knew straight away. I could tell. I mean you can tell with children ... I always do as soon as I know he is ill. I call the doctor as soon as he is poorly. I knew he was ill and needed to see a doctor.

Mothers were sometimes reluctant to seek medical advice or delayed consultation because they thought that they were 'pestering' the doctor.

It was a Tuesday afternoon and there was no surgery. It would have been a call out and I wasn't that worried.

Because I like to be fair. I thought I would see how she got on. She didn't seem to get worse ... She didn't seem in danger so I didn't like to pester the doctor. I could cope – I wasn't panicking.

The decision not to consult was sometimes justified by the fact that mothers felt confident that they could deal with an illness or that an illness was self-limiting and consultation was therefore neither necessary nor worthwhile as there was no 'cure'.

You can't take anything for colds and viruses. I was giving her Calpol and cough medicine.

I didn't think there was anything they could give her.

I have approached them before about being sick and he [the doctor] just says starve them and give them plenty of drinks. They haven't given me anything for it before.

Because I have consulted them before about coughs and it is a waste of time. He [the doctor] is more interested in me smoking. He didn't give her a prescription or anything.

Part of the monitoring period coincided with a 'flu epidemic and media coverage affected some mothers' consultation behaviour. (It was interesting to note, however, that a whole range of conditions were assigned the 'flu label by mothers. Children with vomiting and diarrhoea were reported as having 'flu, as were children suffering from ear infections.)

Well, with it being on the telly – just go to bed and take paracetamols. They don't seem to be giving anything else.

In summary, although the decision to consult was mainly taken in view of the nature, severity and duration of the child's condition, other factors were also important in relation to particular conditions or certain children. There was, however, little evidence that maternal employment affected the decision to consult.

Mothers face a dilemma with regard to the consultation decision; seeking medical attention for trivial illness is frowned upon but failing to seek advice could be dangerous. The decision to consult relies very heavily on the mother's interpretation of clinical and other signs and self-reports by her young child. Mothers may err on the side of caution, but as one mother commented, 'you don't mess about with kids'; to delay too long, in extreme cases, could prove fatal.

THE DOCTOR/PATIENT ENCOUNTER

Staying at home with a child while the doctor called or accompanying the child to the doctor's surgery were mainly the responsibility of the child's mother. In 85% of episodes the mother alone accompanied the child. In 5% of cases the father alone stayed with the child or attended the surgery. In 5% of episodes both parents were with the child and in the remaining 5% of cases, a grandmother or someone else took the child to the doctor's.

Most of the mothers reported that, apart from medicines, their doctor had not advised any treatment. A few mentioned strategies to reduce temperatures or rehydrate the child.

He said with a virus antibiotics are no good. Just sponging him down and turning off the heating in the house. I was freezing on Friday night. Him roasting and me cold.

Sometimes the fact the doctor was unable to offer any 'cure' was disappointing for parents.

I gave her Benylin at first, but that didn't seem to move it, so I gave her Boots' Nirolex. But the doctor said don't give her anything, it will clear up on its own. He didn't seem to have much time.

Sometimes the advice offered by the GP was difficult for mothers to carry out or there was a definite gap in communications.

Just a high fibre diet. Well, she wasn't overkeen. She likes fruit but I think I have overdone it. I think I have put her off. It is on and off. I can't keep it on all the time – she gets fed up with it. It is quite difficult to keep this diet up for a long period.

[for croup] He said something about hanging wet clothes, but I don't know what he meant so I didn't do it anyway.

He said gargle with salt and water. I didn't try. I thought he was too upset.

[antibiotic] It tastes horrible. I have trouble getting it down him – I've stopped giving it to him because it is so horrible – I made him have it at first.

Despite these problems, most mothers were generally satisfied with the service they received from their GP. At the end of the monitoring period mothers were asked to review the past year and rate their satisfaction with their doctor: 38% said they felt very satisfied and 43% were quite satisfied with their GP, while 8% were uncertain and the rest had more definite reservations, 4% being fairly dissatisfied and 7% very unsatisfied.

There were some problems in interpreting these figures, however, as some mothers who had seemed to express satisfaction by choosing the 'quite satisfied' option then went on to justify this choice by making negative comments. When mothers were asked to explain their rating, the first two responses they gave were coded. Some mothers only gave one response so a total of 191 responses was recorded: 63% of these were positive evaluations of their GPs while 37% were negative. The reasons identified for the generally high level of satisfaction with GP services were mainly concerned with access, general friendliness, the quality of the encounter with the doctor and diagnosis and treatment.

With regard to access, there were 27 positive comments from mothers and 15 negative ones. Sometimes mothers complained that they had difficulty getting an appointment at all, some that they had difficulty getting to see a particular doctor and some had difficulties getting to the surgery.

> When they had the measles I had to get another doctor out because he [own GP] always says, 'Bring them up'. But at that time I couldn't. They were really bad about that.

> Because if she has been really bad they have been all right. If I have wanted an appointment I have managed to get one.

> There are three doctors there, that is the problem – you never see the same one.

Mothers in paid employment were no more likely to complain about access than mothers who were at home.

Nine mothers specifically mentioned the friendliness of their GP and other surgery staff although two were critical of this. The most frequently mentioned positive comments about the service from GPs related to the quality of the encounter with the doctor. In 27 instances mothers mentioned that their doctors listened or examined their child thoroughly; however, 12 comments were critical of their doctors in these respects. Further, while there were 12 positive comments about the diagnosis and treatment of disease, there were 18 critical comments about this. Mothers were particularly critical of doctors who prescribed too quickly or who failed to communicate effectively with parents.

> They are very helpful. They just don't shove you in and send you out. But here they go through everything with you.

> Because he explains things to you if it is something quite obscure and doesn't always rush to give you a prescription.

> He always listens and gives him a right good check over when I go.

> I wouldn't say I was really unsatisfied but some have the prescription written out for you before you get in the door.

> I very rarely see our own doctor, more often than not I see one of the others. There is one that they tend to put you with if it is a child and we're generally unsatisfied – if you

go you generally have a prescription waiting for you before you say what it is.

Ten times we went then ended up having to go to another surgery. He was choking and no-one would tell us what was wrong. It was asthma – the other doctor sent him straight away for an X-ray. He had a shadow on his lung.

Five mothers specifically mentioned that their doctor was 'good' with children and no mothers were critical of their GP in this respect.

He is a lovely child doctor. He is better with children than with adults. If it is a child he will do anything.

About a third of the sample said that they would like their doctors to give them more information about their child's health.

While the service offered by doctors was mainly evaluated positively, several mothers claimed that during the past year they had had some bad experience with a doctor. Indeed, some mothers who gave positive evaluations of the service qualified this by saying 'It depends who you see'. Seventeen percent claimed that whilst attending the doctor's with their child during the last year, they felt that the doctor had 'tried to get rid of them'. Twenty-seven percent thought that there had been an occasion when the doctor seemed too busy to spend enough time with them. Fourteen percent of mothers in the sample claimed that they had been given the impression on at least one occasion that the doctor did not care about them and 6% described other 'bad' experiences at their doctor's. Again complaints about GPs were not confined to any particular social group and responses to these questions did not differ between working and non-working mothers.

We next asked if doctor consultation related to any other aspects of a mother's behaviour. The direction of causation is problematic but, for example, if a child visited the GP was he or she more likely to be given medicines? Did the fact that a child consulted relate to the types of treatment and nursing the child received? For example, were children more likely to be kept indoors or away from other children if they had seen a doctor? Further, while maternal employment did not significantly affect consultation rates, was it a factor which influenced other aspects of child health care?

MEDICATIONS, DOCTOR CONSULTATION
AND MATERNAL EMPLOYMENT

In most of the episodes of illness followed up at Phase II of the research the child was given some form(s) of medication, either prescribed by the GP or bought over the counter at the chemist's. In only about a sixth of the episodes was no medication given. Many children were given several medications: for example, a child with a cough was frequently given both an analgesic or antipyretic and a 'cough bottle'. Only the first three medications given to the child were recorded so our figures to some extent underestimate the scale and range of medications children were given.

In all, children were given analgesics/antipyretics (usually the proprietary brand known as 'Calpol') in 57% of the episodes in the monitoring phase of the research. In 26% of episodes, antibiotics were prescribed, in 20% of cases the child was given cough medicines and in 35% of episodes some other form of symptom relief such as kaolin and morphine (for diarrhoea) was given. In 3% of cases other types of medication were mentioned.

While in 17% of episodes all the medication given to the child was prescribed, in 24% of episodes children were given both prescribed and proprietary brands and in 37% of all episodes children were given just medicines which had been bought over the counter in the chemist's or grocer's.

If the doctor had been consulted it was slightly more likely that the child would be given some form of medication. However the majority of the children who had not seen a GP were also given medicines. It was less likely that children with vomiting and diarrhoea would be given medicines and it was also less likely that these children would consult; this pattern to some extent explained the small difference in medication use for consulting and non-consulting children. Only for antibiotics was there a significant difference in medication for children who had and who had not consulted: in the 72 episodes where children were given antibiotics, in all but three cases the child had seen the doctor. For these three episodes it may be the case that GPs left a prescription without seeing the child but some mothers, as earlier accounts demonstrate, gave children their brother's or sister's medicine if the mother perceived that all the children in her family had 'come down' with the same type of illness.

For other types of medicines there were only minor differences between children who had and who had not seen a doctor. A child was almost as likely to receive an analgesic, cough bottle or other symptomatic relief bought over the counter as one prescribed by the doctor and, as mentioned earlier, many children were receiving both prescribed and bought medicines at the same time.

There was little difference in the use of medicines between children of mothers at home and those in paid work. Most children were given medicines whether their mother worked or not.

It was also interesting to note that whether a child had seen a doctor or not or whether or not the mother was in paid employment made little difference to the nursing and other strategies mothers adopted to treat their child's illness, relieve distress and prevent the spread of infection.

In 12% of episodes doctors had advised some form of treatment other than medicines. Some doctors recommended strategies to reduce temperatures or to rehydrate, although many mothers took similar measures without the advice of their GP. In 46% of episodes mothers mentioned treatments they had tried apart from medications. A few mothers specifically mentioned measures they had taken to reduce their child's temperature and in around half of the episodes of vomiting and diarrhoea, mothers mentioned restricting food intake. Many home nursing strategies were tried.

Those mothers who used home remedies to relieve their child's symptoms occasionally had doubts about the wisdom of some of the strategies they adopted.

[earache] I gave him Disprol but that didn't seem to help so I gave him some warm olive oil and cotton wool. I am so undecided about that. Someone told me that an emergency doctor had gone mad about it [but] you have to get the child some relief any way you can.

[sore mouth] Ice cream to try to cool it down.

[for 'pike' on eye] I warmed a bit of milk and bathed it – it seemed to bust it.

[diarrhoea] Arrowroot – you don't know what to give kiddies, do you? I boiled her some milk and arrowroot.

Lemon drinks were popular for colds and Indian Brandy for 'tummy upsets'. Treatments for coughs included propping the child up in bed with pillows, steam to ease breathing and, sometimes expensive, ionizers, vaporizers and chest rubs.

I never give him cough stuff. I give him a warm bath. The steam helps him to breathe.

I tried Vicks. I bought a vaporizer thing for £11, but it just made him sick. It didn't help.

Many mothers recognized the value of nursing care, of providing a loving and comfortable environment for their sick child. Many children were moved downstairs onto the settee so that their mothers could 'keep an eye on them' and so that the child could be with its family. Sometimes the children were given a 'light' diet or special foods.

Just kept her warm and kept her in bed. I didn't give her fried things. Soups and that kind of thing and a bit of toast.

In the night I gave her a hot water bottle.

Just keeping her warm and inside and plenty of fluids.

Keeping the child indoors and in bed were very popular home nursing strategies although the reasons for taking these measures were varied. In over half of the episodes (60%) the child was in bed or 'down on the settee' for at least a short time during the illness. In 34% of these episodes the child lay down during the day for just a few hours, in 22% of these episodes for about a day, in 30% for two or three days and in the remaining episodes the child was bedridden for more than three days. There was no clear link between doctor consultation and the fact that the child was on bed rest. It seemed that adopting the 'sick role' was expected of the child who was deemed ill and this implied 'lying down' or resting for at least a few hours. Similarly, if children were 'ill' they were kept indoors and again it seemed that this was connected with the child fulfilling a sick role. In almost two thirds of the episodes, irrespective of doctor consultation or maternal employment, children were kept in during their illness. This action did not clearly relate to either the nature or severity of the child's condition, although this was the reason given in 37% of episodes. As in the case of disease causality, it was difficult to separate out the various strands in the justifications for behaviour. Although the first reason for keeping a child indoors might relate to the nature of the child's condition, there were often other factors to consider. For example, the weather was often cited as a reason for keeping a child indoors as it was perceived that certain types of weather were likely to exacerbate illnesses, particularly in the case of coughs and colds. Children with temperatures were also seen as susceptible to 'chills' or 'picking up' other conditions if they were exposed to the elements.

> Just because it was cold and foggy out and with a cold it is not the best thing.

> As far as the earache goes I'd keep her indoors. Cold wind aggravates earache.

> Apart from anything else it was foul weather and because she had a temperature I didn't want to add insult to injury by taking her out in wet, windy weather.

> I think he was a bit wobbly. He was quite weakened by it and I was worried about him catching a chill. Just that day. If they have a good night's sleep they are OK.

> I have to do anyway if it is damp – it just goes straight on his chest. Although the doctors say he should lead a normal life I don't think he can really. We have loads of problems with him if it is really cold. They [at school] seem to let them play out in the damp and wet. I've been up to say that [child] can't with his chest.

The fact that a child was coughing was also seen as a justification for keeping her indoors. This was sometimes because a change in temperature – moving from outdoors to indoors – was thought to induce coughing, but children's outdoor behaviour was also perceived as a factor which could lead to coughing attacks.

With her having a chest complaint I thought it best to keep her indoors. I don't like her playing out. She comes in coughing – if she runs around it can start it off.

Well, with that sort of thing [cough] she had got it is best to keep them at one temperature, in one place.

Keeping children 'warm' was sometimes perceived as a factor which aided recovery and prevented more serious conditions developing. Keeping a child warm demanded that they be kept indoors.

Well, I thought if he was chesty and unwell – to keep him warm in case he gets pneumonia.

In 18% of all episodes mothers mentioned severe or changeable weather as a reason for keeping a child indoors. Six percent specifically mentioned that the child 'had a temperature' as if this in itself explained their decision to keep their child in. In around 3% of episodes mothers specifically mentioned that they did not want their child 'running around'. Other reasons given for keeping a child indoors were partly punitive. If a child was suspected of 'shamming' they would not be allowed the normal privileges of 'leisure time'; they could not go out as this implied 'playing out'. Other mothers also mentioned the idea that if children were off school and therefore their illness was 'official', they could not play out and the sick role was accordingly enforced. The child was expected to act 'ill' and this implied staying in, being passive, avoiding other children and, for a short time at least, lying prostrate either in bed or on the sofa.

If they are off school they have to stay indoors. That is a rule of the house.

[where the child was suspected of feigning] Apart from as a punishment.

I wouldn't let her play out with her being off school and I put her to bed early. I didn't let her get away with it.

I did it because I thought if he thought he could get away with it he would always be off. Not because he was poorly.

If they are ill they can't play out for me. No work, no play.

Sometimes mothers were unable to keep their child in despite the fact that they would have liked to have done so. In the following three accounts mothers' work commitments meant that they had to take their children out for a short time.

Well, I thought he would be better to be kept in a warm room. I didn't want him to go out in the cold. But it wasn't possible because his Grandma had him and she had to do her shopping.

She went to the childminder's and she had to go out with her. I probably would have kept her in if she had been with me.

[after tonsillectomy] They [hospital staff] said to keep him in completely for a full week but for me to go to work he had to go to my mum's. But I put a scarf round – she only lives across the road. He is not a kid you can keep in. By the middle of the week I let his friend come in to play with him.

Occasionally the nature of the child's condition meant that the child needed to stay near home. Children with diarrhoea were kept in in case they needed 'to dash'. The following account was from an interview with a mother whose child had cystitis.

I thought it was a chill and it was cold outside. Not only that, he might have wee'd himself.

Worry that the child would spread infection was also mentioned as a reason for keeping a child indoors. In all, in 32% of episodes mothers considered that they needed to keep their child away from other children. This was mainly to prevent the spread of infection – this was mentioned in 81% of these episodes. Occasionally this was on the advice of the GP. However, several mothers isolated their child because of fears that their child would be exposed to further threats of illness if in contact with other children. Some conditions, such as diarrhoea or vomiting, were more likely to lead to isolation (although this was not always the case) but coughs and colds were also regarded as conditions that children could 'pass on' to others. Sometimes preventing the spread of infection was seen as a moral responsibility by mothers.

I didn't want anybody else's child getting it. I had to tell people. I had to keep away from friends with young children.

Because I didn't want their mothers to go through what I was going through.

Well, if it were infectious or if she was starting with anything else. In case she passed it on or if she was going to get something else on top of it.

Well, so that he didn't pass on the bug.

That is why I have not sent him in [to school] – coughing germs in the classroom.

Although mothers sometimes perceived that isolating the child was desirable, avoiding contact with other children, especially other family members, was almost impossible to achieve. In 16% of episodes where mothers thought it was necessary to isolate their child they found it difficult to do so.

It is physically impossible when you have got three others at home.

Her sister had had an operation. I was worried about her getting it [flu] – and she has, but there was nothing I could do. I rang the hospital to try to find out how she could avoid it. But there was nothing I could do.

In the following account, a mother describes how the nature of her work meant that isolating her sick child was impossible. This mother also suggests that preventing the spread of infection is a two-way process: while mothers must keep their sick children away from healthy ones, it is also the responsibility of other parents to keep their healthy children away from a sick child to avoid the 'risk' of illness.

I didn't want to spread it around . . . [but] with me being a childminder – mums are reluctant to take time off work when my children are ill. They would rather risk their own child getting it. With taking them down to school I had to take [sick child] out.

Although many mothers claimed that they isolated their child during illness episodes, deciding whether or not a condition was contagious was sometimes problematic. Deciding the means whereby disease was spread was also a complicated issue.

> She has been coughing and sneezing all over, but she puts her hand over her mouth so there has been no necessity to keep her away from other children. She hasn't been spreading germs that way.

It was often the case that other family members were ill at the same time as the child. In more than a third of the episodes at Phase II (38%) mothers claimed that several family members were ill. In 45% of these episodes it was the mother herself who was ill and in the remaining cases, other children or the child's father. Several members of the family succumbing to illness at the same time created a range of additional problems in the management of the illness episode. The chief problem which emerged for mothers was the amount of extra work this involved – running up and down stairs and piles of extra washing. As several mothers pointed out, ill children tend to be irritable and bicker with each other and there could be problems keeping them 'entertained'. If the mother was ill herself it meant even greater strain.

> Well, I was sick myself. How was I going to cope with him being sick as well. Who was going to take [brother] to school? Who would get the shopping? Would I get any sleep? I couldn't cope ... It cost me a fortune in videos. Then [brother] got sick as well but he wasn't as bad.

> [mother ill] In the night I couldn't sleep. You get ratty. Only that, well, it has made it difficult. All I wanted to do was go to sleep.

> He was feeling better when I was feeling rotten. I just wasn't well enough and he wanted something to eat and I just didn't want to be bothered.

> Only that I had two sick children at home at the same time and it was very difficult for me ... it was difficult splitting the attention.

> [his brother] was in hospital at the same time. I needed to be in two places at one time. I needed to cut myself in half.

It was worse. A lot of extra work on. They were all bickering and arguing. I am getting symptoms now, not as bad, but I don't like to give in.

Occasionally others in the family being ill at the same time made matters easier for the mother. If a sibling was ill it might mean that problems associated with collecting a well child from school were avoided.

Sometimes children's illnesses meant that the mother was virtually housebound if she thought that her child was not well enough to go out.

It was just a bit awkward. I had [brother] at home as well. My mother had to come over in a taxi while I took [child] to the doctor's. I had no-one else here to look after him.

Most mothers reacted stoically to the problems associated with dealing with additional work, or the strain of being ill at the same time as their child. Similarly, mothers whose children were ill during the night reacted dispassionately to having disturbed sleep; vomiting at night meant bed changes, children up coughing could cause a great deal of anxiety as well as making a disturbing noise, worry that the child might become worse meant that mothers lay half awake listening for any unusual signs. Some mothers admitted that this made them feel worn out.

I was worried to death so I didn't mind [being up]. I was shattered actually. I hung around – I had a pretty rough night. I was dead on my legs the next day.

I always hear the kids. They only turn over and I am awake. Two nights I had to get up with her, the rest of the time I was just listening.

No, no problems really. Just a bit of backache from balancing on the edge of a single bed.

Although the demands of work meant that mothers might have to get up early after a disturbed night, the problems associated with being 'shattered' were by no means confined to mothers in paid work. The second of the following accounts demonstrates that during the stressful time of illness, work could offer some relief from the demands of home.

> We were awake most of the night. One night I had to be up at 6. If you had seen me at work. I thought I was dying.

> Weeks! It went on for weeks. Every hour or two hours during the night we were up. Six weeks and we never got a decent night's sleep. I was literally dropping. I don't know how I managed to carry on working. I kept working just to get out. I would have gone mad otherwise.

Whether the mother was up during the night, whether the child rested during the day, whether the child was given medicines and whether the child was isolated were not clearly related to illness severity, doctor consultation or maternal employment. It seems that if a child was absent from school – that is, once the child had been deemed 'ill' – the mother adopted strategies for dealing with the illness which were perceived as appropriate to either serious or more trivial illnesses. The sick role was to some extent imposed on the child and this did not relate to the nature of the disease or its severity. The child would, in most cases, be given some kind of medicine, would be kept indoors and would be expected to rest. It was also expected that the child would fulfil the sick role by co-operating with these strategies: 'playing out', for example, was frowned upon. Being ill meant being bedridden, housebound, passive and quiet – at least for a few hours! For some, absence from school implied a certain ritual – no school, no play. In some households this was given the status of a rule. If a child was feigning it was assumed that s/he would not enjoy performing most aspects of the sick role, apart from school avoidance, and strategies were therefore adopted to ensure that if a child was suspected of feigning they would not 'get away with it'.

In our study, although doctor consultation did relate to the nature and severity of the disease, it was not associated with maternal employment or social class. The many other strategies mothers adopted to treat illness and relieve their child's distress were not related to either doctor consultation or maternal employment (except for the prescription of antibiotic drugs).

Drawing on a study of preventive health care for preschool children, Mayall (1986) suggests that:

All mothers of whatever class background were highly motivated, positive and interventionist. This adds up to an impressive picture of a responsible approach to preventive child health care.

Our own findings suggest that the measures mothers took during sickness to treat their child's diseases and to relieve symptoms and distress similarly add up to an impressive picture of the caring and health work provided by mothers to nurse their sick children back to health.

7

Child health care and women's employment

So far, most of the material in the book has focused on the impact of women's employment on child health care. In this chapter the question is turned around and we examine the effects of children's illnesses and the provision of care on women's work. Some of the potential effects of child health care on women's employment were addressed indirectly in Chapters 1 and 3. It was pointed out in the latter that mothers in our sample had selected themselves into particular types of employment, predominantly into jobs which were low skill, part-time and nearby, in order to ease the problems associated with providing child care during periods of both child health and illness. The complicated networks mothers were involved in to provide substitute care during school holidays were also described and Chapter 5 outlined the even more complicated arrangements mothers often made to provide child care in the event of illness episodes.

In this chapter, we describe the ways in which home and work responsibilities are reconciled from the point of view of the mother as an employee. What happens when mothers are forced to take time off work? Do working mothers 'take advantage' of employers by taking time off and possibly misleading employers about the reasons for their absence? How much time do mothers take off work for child illness within the context of other work absence? How do employers react to work absence arising from children's illnesses? Work absence bears costs – work may be disrupted, expensive replacement labour may be necessary, deadlines may not be met and yet wages may still have to be paid. Who bears these financial costs of children's illness episodes: is it employers that are being short-changed by parents or do families bear these costs? There are other non-pecuniary costs associated with work absence: possible loss of face or reputation for the employee, reduced opportunities for promotion if the employee is regarded as 'unreliable' and increased family stress. We examine these issues within the context of family life and look at whether these costs are borne by the mother alone or are shared within families.

The issue of work absence for children's illness is a difficult one, both as an employment issue and as a moral dilemma faced in thousands of homes in Britain every day.

It is just what you put first. Do you put your children first or your job? The choice can be hard.

The introductory chapter describes the provision of leave for family responsibilities within the EEC and elsewhere in the West. Britain has a poor record in comparison with other European nations. In short, there is no statutory entitlement to leave, paid or otherwise, for family responsibilities in Britain. There are pockets of provision: for example, some local authorities have contractual arrangements which allow leave for fathers following the birth of a child. Such 'paternity leave' may be paid or unpaid. Some large employers have formal arrangements for 'compassionate leave' following bereavement or serious family crises; these may be discretionary and may be unpaid. However, few employers have any formal arrangements for paid or unpaid leave for parents in the case of children's illness.

As far as our own sample was concerned, entitlement to compassionate leave in the case of children's illness was scarce. It may have been that mothers were unaware that such leave was available to them. This is doubtful. Amongst part-time workers particularly, entitlement to paid sick leave was patchy, so there is little likelihood of a leave entitlement for family responsibilities. Only two mothers mentioned that they were entitled to take compassionate, paid leave in the case of their child becoming ill. In more than half of the sample of those in paid work, mothers said that there were no arrangements, either formal or informal, for them to take time off work if their child was ill. In almost all of the rest of the sample the arrangements to take time off during children's illness were informal. Nine percent of mothers mentioned that they could take their work home if necessary or could take their child in with them to work and that they would do this rather than taking time off. Thirty percent of mothers said that they could swap shifts with colleagues or make time up on other days. Four percent of mothers said that they saved holidays for such illness episodes and could take holiday at short notice. Thirty four percent of the women said that these informal arrangements had been an important consideration when taking their current job.

Mothers were also asked whether they would be paid for taking time off if their child was ill. Sixty percent said that they would lose pay. Some of the other 40% only avoided losing pay by taking work home or making up the time later. At the initial interview mothers were also asked about what they thought their employer's attitude was to parents taking time off to look after their children. In 45% of cases mothers thought that their employer would be sympathetic if employees were forced to take time off to care for a sick child; but again it should be remembered here that many mothers did not anticipate that they would have real 'time off' but would instead seek to swap shifts or make up time. These descriptions of positive attitudes in employers may have referred to general arrangements made during children's illness episodes rather than perceptions about taking time off as such. Nonetheless, many mothers were grateful to their employers for their understanding. A surprising number of mothers mentioned that attitudes tended to depend on whether their 'boss' had children of his or her own.

> He is a family man. He will go out of his way to assist you if he can.

> The boss has just had a new baby, so they know. They are very understanding.

> He has a little girl of his own. I don't think he would mind. I wouldn't get paid for the time but he is a pretty easygoing chap. I wouldn't usually take time off, my mum would look after him.

There again, they always try to meet everybody's needs. When I was off someone else was off the next day and they rang me up, so I covered for someone else and made the hours up.

Employers were perceived as being unequivocally unsympathetic in around a fifth of the sample (22%). Twelve percent of mothers did not know what the reaction of their employer would be as they had not broached the issue and had not yet taken time off. Where a fairly sympathetic attitude was described, it was sometimes qualified by provisos, such as, it depends on the severity or it depends on the duration of the illness. In general, provided a child was extremely ill, the illness was of short duration and only occurred once, even the most hardened employers were sympathetic.

I don't think he would mind the odd couple of times, but I don't think he'd like it on a regular . . .

They prefer you to have as little time as possible, but I suppose if it is an emergency . . .

Understanding, providing it is only short term. By short term I mean a day.

In 13% of the sample the mother was employed by a relative and therefore expected a sympathetic response. It became clear from verbatim comments by mothers that the response of the 'employer' depended very much on informal agreements with her line manager rather than the response being a reflection of 'company policy'.

What the ––– Building Society and what my manager thinks might be two completely different things. My manager would be all right about it.

My manager is very good. I don't know what the bank feels as a whole.

Well, I don't know about the company itself . . . the manageress takes it on herself. [last time] I couldn't afford to lose a day's pay, so she said 'Don't worry, we will arrange a swap'.

It was also clear that the mothers had selected themselves into jobs where their expectations of employers during illness episodes were low. In the following account a mother demonstrates that although her employer would be reasonably sympathetic in an emergency, an informal condition of employment was that the mother should make other arrangements rather than expecting any time off:

... When she interviewed me for the job she asked me whether there was anyone who could look after [child] if she was ill. I said yes, because her grandparents are just in the village. But if she was very ill she wouldn't expect me to go in.

They normally ask you [before you get the job] what would you do if your children were ill, how would you get into work?

They think that when you take the job that you will make arrangements, that was something they asked you when I applied for the job.

For a few mothers the prospect of taking time off with or without pay was not on the cards.

He hates it. It is just a nuisance.

If I had no holidays left I would have to be sick myself. They are making it really so that you have to lie. I don't think they like it, I'm sure they don't. The first time I rang in she wasn't very pleased.

At the initial study interview, if this was applicable, mothers were also asked about their partner taking time off work and the attitude of their partner's employer to parents taking time off. In 87% of cases mothers said that they did not remember their partner taking time off work for this reason. In 8% of cases mothers reported that their partner very occasionally took time off and in 5% of cases that taking time off was shared or the father was more likely to take time off than the mother. In more than a third of cases (36%) mothers were unaware of whether their partner's employer would be sympathetic to a parent taking time off during illness – presumably because the issue was perceived as irrelevant or had not arisen since the father had never taken time off for this reason. Around a fifth of fathers were self-employed and so again the issue had not arisen. For the rest, partners' employers were described in 28% of cases as sympathetic and in 17% as unsympathetic. Again, where the employer was described as sympathetic, this may have been qualified by provisos associated with the severity and duration of the illness. Similarly, an 'understanding' attitude did not preclude loss of pay or holidays.

I don't think he would tolerate it over a long period of time but I think he would be pretty understanding if it was just an odd day.

I don't think they are against it. They would dock his pay or expect him to take leave.

They wouldn't really allow it. He even had to put in for his holidays at the time I was having the babies.

It's not really that kind of place.

I think they would take a very dim view of it.

I don't think he would be particularly upset provided it wasn't for a prolonged period. With being out on the road it is not detrimental, you soon make up the time again.

So, at the outset of the research project mothers had low expectations of employers. Their employer was likely to be reasonably sympathetic if their child was rarely ill, was seriously ill and the illness was shortlived. Mothers mainly expected to receive no pay if they took time off. Those who reported no loss of earnings usually expected to have to catch up in some way: to make the time up by working harder or by covering for another colleague in a similar kind of emergency.

TAKING TIME OFF WORK

When asked retrospectively about their child's last illness, around a quarter of mothers reported that they had taken time off work (26%) while in 62% of cases mothers had avoided taking time off by arranging for substitute child care or swapping work arrangements. In the remaining cases the question of time off had not arisen; for example, the child might have become ill during a family holiday. All mothers who had taken time off explained the reason for their absence to their employer; no mothers used the excuse that they themselves were ill. Twelve percent of mothers lost pay and 6% lost holidays. In six cases fathers took time off, in three cases partners were self-employed and in one case the absence was for less than a day.

However, the retrospective data was judged as unreliable in terms of estimating the actual amount of time parents took off work to care for sick children. This was for several reasons, the main one being that mothers were being asked to remember an illness that may have occurred several months before. When asked retrospectively about their child's illness record, mothers tended to recall more serious episodes of malaise rather than coughs or colds. Figures may not therefore have been representative of work absence during more trivial illnesses and may thus have overestimated the amount of leave usually taken.

The main part of the study, carried out retrospectively over two school terms, was therefore seen as providing a more reliable estimate of work absence. Children who were absent from school were followed up within two weeks of the episode occurring. Mothers' recollections were fresh and accurate. Nevertheless, in this case the figures reported are likely to underestimate time off work as we only followed up illness which led to school absence. Children may have been ill at the weekend or during school holidays and this may have led to work absence for parents although we were not able to monitor or record this. As far as fulltime working mothers are concerned the figures are likely to be fairly accurate as most worked a normal Monday–Friday week. The figures are likely to be less accurate for those mothers working weekend shifts.

It has often been assumed that mothers of young children have high levels of work absence and that their excess absence can be accounted for by childhood illness. The findings from our study do not support this. Over the seven months covered by the study (which included the winter period when childhood illnesses are very much more common), the working mothers lost an average of less than one day each (0.9 work days) in order to provide health care for the study's target child. (This is in fact something of an overestimate, since the loss of a 'day' for part-time workers may not mean the loss of eight hours' work.)

When illness in non-study children was taken into account, the absence figure rose to 1.2 work days per mother. Over the same period, the mothers took an average of 4.7 days for their own sickness absence although excluding three mothers who had very long absences reduced this figure to 2.1 days per mother. Additional leave for other family reasons such as funerals or to cope with domestic emergencies such as the kitchen roof falling in accounted for an additional 0.3 days per mother. Very approximately, therefore, child health care accounted for no more than a third of mothers' absence from work figures. Further, in some cases leave for care of an ill child was offset by a reduction in annual leave.

In the majority of illness episodes mothers did not take any time off work. It was difficult to be precise about the actual number of episodes which involved time off, as some mothers made up time at a later stage, but of those that did take time off the duration of leave was usually short. On only three occasions did a mother take more than four days off work for any one episode. Overall, a third (33%) of working mothers took a day or more off work over the seven months monitoring period.

It was interesting to note that there was no clear link between the number of illness episodes a child suffered and the total amount of time that a mother took off work, or indeed whether the mother took any time off at all. This was because in most cases mothers managed to avoid any time off and also because time off was influenced by other factors such as whether the mother had reliable help available in case of childhood illness. For example, a child that had six separate episodes of illness only resulted in two days off work for the mother. Two thirds of those mothers that had taken time off work also claimed that they had had help from relatives. In the combined sample of full and part-time workers, mothers' work absence was lower among those women whose own mother lived nearby. Looking more closely, however, revealed different patterns in the full and part-time workers: part-timers were much more likely to have had work absence if their own mother did not live nearby, but no relationship was now apparent within the group of fulltime workers.

Thus work absence was dependent on a variety of factors – school absence, inflexible working conditions and lack of alternative support – and these factors might be different on different occasions for a working mother. Because the great majority of mothers in our study had members of their family living nearby, it was difficult to assess whether not having such support made any difference to mothers' work absence. There was a tendency for mothers who did not have the maternal grandmother nearby to take more time off work, but this finding did not reach statistical significance.

For fathers or partners the amount of time lost from work due to illness in the target child was very low. In nine episodes (of 282) the father did take some time off: this involved six fathers (four of these fathers were self-employed). However, during four of the episodes the time off was less than a full day. In one case the father took 11 days leave for illness in the study child but this was because the child fell ill at the end of a family holiday abroad and the family were unable to return. Even including this one long absence episode, the mean amount of leave taken by fathers over the study period was only just over 0.1 days per father – perhaps an hour each over seven months. Again, this figure may underestimate the actual extent of leave because it does not cover weekends or school holidays. About a quarter of fathers were reported to have taken some other leave for family reason – funerals, caring for an ill partner, taking Grandma to the hospital and so on. This absence was usually short and amounted to a mean of less than half a day absence per father over the study period.

The fact that so many mothers were able to sustain work during children's illnesses was perhaps a reflection of the commitment of mothers to their work. Whether to stay at home to care for a sick child or whether to go into work was never an easy decision for mothers: they were worried if they did go into work but were guilty if they missed work. Further, as a mother in one of the following accounts notes, when she did take time off to care for a sick child it led to feelings of guilt when she herself became ill. In the case recorded, the mother did not feel she could take time off for her own illness.

Chapter 6 notes that it was common for illness in the study child to be associated with illness in other family members, which would intensify the dilemma for working mothers.

My main worry was that I had to go to work and what would I do? . . . I was having nightmares all night. Just the hassle. Just knowing that I couldn't be here [with child].

It was difficult but I thought, well he [child] is more important. My only worry was that someone would have to work over in my place – I felt guilty about that.

I felt a bit guilty about being off again but he comes first. Then I became ill myself. That adds to it. But if you get the sack you get the sack, that is it.

The usual worries. Will he be all right for Monday? When am I going to make my hours up? I would take holiday but I have run out.

There was a commitment I was missing, I felt very concerned about missing work. I was ill the week later and I felt very reluctant to take time off the following week. I went in.

Those mothers that managed to arrange alternative care for their child might avoid some of the guilt in relation to work but might nevertheless be troubled by the fact that they could not care for their child themselves.

With the hours I do, unless it is drastic, it is difficult to get time off. I was worried when I was at work even though she wasn't all that poorly.

I came straight home from work on the dot. I usually work longer. My work was mounting up, I knew that I would have to catch up. This time it was easy because my sister was on the spot. I breathed a sigh of relief, I was really lucky she was left in capable hands.

If mothers were forced to take time off work to care for their sick child they frequently had to explain the reason for their absence to their employer. Occasionally mothers with flexible work patterns could avoid what was often an embarrassing situation.

They didn't realize I had been off. The nature of my work means that I can come and go as I please. I could make up the work later.

On all but one occasion where mothers had to explain their absence to their employer they gave the true reason. There is often an assumption that mothers use the excuse of their own illness to explain time off to care for their sick child. We found virtually no evidence to support this. Mothers told the truth and as a result, even if employers were sympathetic, frequently suffered loss of earnings or holidays.

I told them that [child] had had an accident. They said go and get him and stay off with him. They were really good about it. We were just so busy I didn't really want to be off.

I just said that [child] had got the flu. I work with old people and I don't want to give it to them. If I had had any holidays I would have taken it, but I had none left.

I told him my little one was poorly. I don't have much time off and I stand in for others so I don't have any problems.

There was just one occasion where a mother felt she could not reveal the true reason for her absence from work.

I told him that I had been ill myself. Employers should be more aware that mothers have to take time off – but that is in an ideal world. It would have been out of the question to give the real reason, it wouldn't have been well received at all.

PAYING THE PRICE FOR TIME OFF WORK

If mothers were unable to make alternative arrangements, or if they preferred to care for their child themselves, the cost of the resulting work absence usually fell upon them rather than their employers. Of the 35 occasions when mothers explained absence to their employer on account of the target child being ill, they lost pay on 20 of these and lost holiday time on nine more. In other words, although employers suffered a certain amount of disruption as a result of childhood illness episodes, they bore the direct, financial costs of illness episodes in just over 3% of cases.

On five occasions fathers were said to have lost some pay although this may have been because they missed work as a self-employed person and were unable to earn, rather than there being an actual deduction by an employer. In some families, particularly if the father was self-employed and was perceived as being in an 'easier' position to take time off, the decision was fraught.

He cancelled a job he was going to do for somebody. It was a real dilemma. I didn't know who should take the day off. It is difficult – he lost a day's work, he will have to make up the time on another day. I didn't know whether I should be the one to go in. I was standing in for someone so I thought I would be letting them down.

The issue of possible loss of pay arose whether or not a mother decided to take time off work. If she did take time off, the loss of earnings could occasionally have serious implications for her family and for those mothers that decided to go into work the decision was sometimes made on account of fear of reduced earnings.

It would be easier financially if they did give you pay when your children are poorly. Then you could take time off without hesitation.

[Lost about £80 pay] It was a nuisance with Christmas – I had plans for that money.

If I am ill I get half pay, but I lost my pay with the children being ill – about £22. My wage usually pays for the food at the weekend. We didn't go without but we had to cut down. My husband's wage is spoken for with the mortgage and bills. It doesn't affect my husband's wage, it affects mine. If it wasn't for my mum and sisters I wouldn't be able to work at all.

It was surprising that no mothers complained about loss of pay – they expected a reduction in earnings. Where they did receive pay it was seen as a bonus and may have been a special 'favour' by the line manager.

I just told him that [child] had been poorly. I think he fiddled it and put it down that I was ill so that I wouldn't lose pay.

Similarly, mothers expected to use holiday for children's illness and saved holiday up deliberately to 'cover' this. However, the main costs of children's illnesses as far as mothers were concerned were physical and psychological. The physical effects of children's illnesses on mothers have already been described and applied to mothers working in the home or in paid employment. Mothers described being tired out, being ill themselves and having sleepless or disturbed nights with their ill child. For those mothers working night shifts there were additional problems. These mothers deliberately opted to work nights in order to look after their children before and after school. If the child was off school sick then mothers were expected to cope regardless of the fact that they may have spent the previous night at work.

> It affected my work in that I didn't get the right sleep. I was working nights and I couldn't cope during the day.

The fact that mothers felt compelled to attend work while 'dead on their feet' may have resulted in poor performance at work and therefore exacted a cost from employers. We could not, of course, measure this.

From the emotional point of view the costs for all mothers of providing child health care were high. Despite the fact that most of the episodes of illness were relatively trivial, they were still worrying for parents. For one mother whose child was extremely ill the worry about her child's condition was devastating. There were also concerns specific to working mothers: they often felt guilty – they could not meet both their home and work responsibilities in the case of illness episodes. They were forced to 'let someone down' – either their work colleagues, their 'boss' or their company, or their family, and in particular and worst of all, their sick child. Arranging alternative care did not always allow mothers to escape from these feelings of unease. Making up time at work or going into work whilst they were ill themselves similarly did not seem to entirely compensate for the disruption caused by missing work. Along with feelings of guilt were feelings of resentment that employers did not appreciate that mothers were occasionally forced to take time off for children's illnesses. They did not expect pay for this time; they simply wanted the reason for absence to be regarded as acceptable. Mothers were aware that in the absence of formal leave for family reasons there was little chance that even reasonably sympathetic employers would look kindly on work absence for reasons of this kind. While particular episodes of absence might be accepted, mothers were aware that explaining their absence could result in loss of face amongst colleagues or reduced chances of promotion. It is seemingly 'well known' that mothers of young children are 'unreliable' employees.

The following accounts explain the attitude of mothers to time off to care for their sick children.

Employers could allow you time off. Not frowned upon – no sideways glances and you are not made to feel guilty at all. I think you shouldn't have to feel guilty at all [or] . . . beholden to your company for letting you have that time off.

If you could just have time off with no pay but your job is still there. But no – you are dumped on when you are part-time.

Children when they are ill want their mums. If you do have to have some time off you should be able to make up the time without the children suffering. I don't expect to get it for nothing – I'd be willing to pay. I'm not going out for luxuries. I am going out because my children are fed and kept warm.

If employers were not just understanding but made a point of saying that they understood. Then you wouldn't feel guilty about saying the children were ill.

For some mothers, the loss of pay involved in taking time off was part of wider problems associated with working part-time, being on low pay and existing on a low income. One mother specifically referred to job status when discussing entitlement to leave and made the distinction between those on the 'staff' and those in more lowly positions. She perceived that there were different informal 'rules' for the two groups. Certainly, as far as our sample was concerned, although the numbers are small and not of statistical significance, those mothers that were able to 'take work home' or were not missed at work tended to be those in more senior positions. Most of the sample, as we have already mentioned, were not 'career' women or in senior positions but women doing manual and clerical jobs.

If you had more family allowance or sick pay, that would be a good thing, then you could afford a night off.

If they would pay people a decent wage then a mother could stay at home and be a proper mum when her children were ill without feeling awful.

Paid leave in case of illness was only part of the solution for many mothers. The difficulty was perceived as stemming from the wider society rather than just associated with employers. Some mothers recognized that it was not 'the done thing' to take time off work irrespective of whether this was formally permissible.

You can get compassionate leave from work, but I feel that if I took that for her being ill I would lose the chance of promotion. You are thought as unreliable. I do know women who do take compassionate leave for that. But I know what is said about them as I am near the manager's desk a lot.

Just for it to be more acceptable for parents to be able to look after their children when they are ill.

. . . a general change in attitude . . . People should realize that if you are a working parent, either a mother or a father, your children have to come first.

While mothers might pay the cost of leave by losing chances of promotion, in the short term the actual feat of managing to arrange alternative child care, make up lost time by extra work, cope with less pay or do without holidays and coping with the guilt associated with leaving a sick child or missing work also exerted a price in terms of maternal stress.

THE PSYCHOLOGICAL COSTS OF THE JUGGLING ACT

In the final interview, mothers completed a short form of the General Health Questionnaire (the GHQ-12), which is a standardized instrument for assessing not general health, as its name suggests, but general psychological distress or well-being. High scores suggest more distress.

A variety of other studies, reviewed by Goldberg and Williams (1988), lead us to expect that mothers of young children would exhibit higher than average GHQ scores. Few direct comparisons are available using the GHQ-12, but the findings of Banks *et al.* (1980) provide some useful context. In their sample of employees in an engineering plant, the mean GHQ-12 score was between 8 and 9 points; unemployed school leavers and other unemployed men had mean scores between 13 and 16. In the present study, the mean of the GHQ-12 scores was 12.3.

Overall GHQ scores were not found to differ significantly amongst the three groups: mean scores for the fulltime workers, part-time workers and mothers who were at home were found to be 12.5, 12.5 and 11.3 respectively.

Two of the most common forms of psychological distress are anxiety and depression and the GHQ-12 includes items relating to both. It became apparent to us from a close look at our data that the lack of an overall difference between groups was obscuring some very interesting patterns on the depression and anxiety items. Longer versions of the GHQ permit proper subscale scores to be calculated for the two conditions, but this is not possible with the GHQ-12.

Recognizing that any findings would have to be treated with caution, we calculated our own 'mini' subscale scores from the items known to be either 'anxiety' or 'depression' items in the large body of published work on the GHQ. We recorded the resulting scores to permit statistical comparisons to be made and looked again at our three groups of mothers.

On the depression measure, we found significant differences between the groups, with mothers at home having the highest scores and fulltime workers the lowest scores. This is in accordance with the findings of other researchers that depressed mood is more common in mothers who are not in paid work.

On the anxiety measure (strictly, 'anxiety and insomnia' because of the content of items in the GHQ-12) fulltime workers had slightly higher scores than the other groups, but this difference did not reach statistical significance.

We next wanted to know if problems in providing child care were statistically related to any of the psychological distress measures, again recognizing that the ones we were using had very considerable limitations. The most interesting finding related to mothers' anxiety levels, where the highest scores were found in fulltime workers who had had to take time off work to care for ill children. Work absence in part-timers was unrelated to their anxiety scores and no patterns were found for the depression measure or the overall GHQ score.

The finding of a relationship between work absence and anxiety scores in fulltime workers must be treated with caution. That said, it was quite a strong relationship and it was not the result of a 'fishing expedition' in which the data were examined in lots of different ways and only the interesting results reported.

The reason for the relationship can only be a matter for speculation. We presume that anxiety scores were not raised by work absence per se, since that might have occurred several months previously, but rather that work absence acts as a marker for a shortage of child care resources that is stress-provoking on an ongoing basis.

ATTITUDES AND SATISFACTION

At the final interview, mothers were also asked in detail about their satisfaction with work in general and about satisfaction with work during episodes of children's illness in particular. Attitudes to work in general were very positive. Work colleagues were described as friendly in 90% of cases. More than two thirds of the mothers disagreed with the statement 'My job is boring'. More than half of the women thought that their job was worthwhile (60%). Only 7% of the working mothers agreed with the statement 'I really dislike my job'.

Although mothers were very positive about work they were less positive about fitting home and work together. Almost 30% said that they worried about home and children when they were at work. (This high level of concern may over-estimate the true picture – because the study was about children's illness, mothers may have referred to those times when their child had been ill.)

Mothers were also very positive about the way that their employer had reacted in case of children's illnesses. When asked how satisfied they felt about the way their employer had reacted to children's illnesses over the past year, only one mother expressed definite dissatisfaction although a further 12% were uncertain. More than half were 'very satisfied' with their employer in this respect. This high level of satisfaction contrasts with the less positive views that mothers had expressed in relation to their employers' general attitudes to leave for family responsibilities. The two sets of findings are not as contradictory as they first appear. It is well established that women experience downward mobility when they return to work after having children and employers know that mothers are prepared to trade a certain amount of flexibility regarding child care against higher wage rates, chances of promotion, etc. Since employers actually bore very little of the costs of childhood illness in our study, the bargain would seem to be quite an advantageous one from their point of view. The reason why women were satisfied with the reaction of employers was that they expected very little from them and indeed were very grateful for small mercies.

If I get the results at work, they are not too bothered about how I achieve it . . . the MD is very considerate . . . the odd time I have taken time off he has been very good about it. Provided I have still sold the same amount, it does not matter.

Combining home and work responsibilities during childhood illness episodes was a far from easy task for mothers in our study. There was very little evidence that mothers 'took advantage' of their employers. The term suggests a level both of dishonesty and of exploitation – mothers were guilty of neither. On only one occasion did a mother feel obliged to mislead her employer about the reasons for her absence and as for exploitation, we have mentioned above that the bargain between mothers and employers tends to be advantageous from the employer's point of view rather than vice versa.

As elsewhere in this book, fathers have played a very small part in this chapter. Several fathers did take time off work to care for their children but they were certainly in the minority. This may be a reflection of traditional societal views of the respective roles of fathers and mothers which were shared by many mothers within our sample. The father was seen as the breadwinner and if one of the parents was forced to jeopardize his or her wages, job or chances of promotion then it made economic sense within most families for it to be the mother to miss work. Further, while it is not generally seen as 'the done thing' for mothers to take time off work to care for a sick child, it was even less so for a father. Within this context most mothers expressed satisfaction with the contribution their partner had made to child health care. Expectations of fathers, like expectations of employers, were low. Mothers had, on the other hand, very high expectations of themselves.

If you take a job you take it on the same terms as a single person. If you can't stand the heat you don't go in the kitchen.

8

Conclusions

We have now described our study and its findings in some detail. The first section of this chapter draws together the main results in order that the reader might see them as part of a pattern, rather than a series of separate findings about schools, doctors, employers and so on.

This summary is structured around nine questions, listed in Chapter 2, which the study was designed to answer.

1. Do children of working mothers have less school absence than children of non-working mothers?

In the Phase I interviews, mothers were asked to recall and provide information about a recent episode of illness in the target child. When these retrospective data were analysed, no significant differences in school absence were found between families where the mother worked fulltime, part-time or did not work outside the home at all. However, a different picture emerged from the prospective data.

In the monitoring phase of the study, 282 illness episodes were identified from school absence records and followed up across the 139 families. (One hundred and ten families had at least one episode.) Of these, 97 were coughs and colds, 37 ears and throats, 60 diarrhoea and/or vomiting and 88 other conditions ranging from boils to swollen eyes and bangs on the head. Two hundred and eleven of the episodes had arisen suddenly, necessitating middle of the night or early morning decision making.

Overall, there was a significant difference in the amount of school absence (as recorded in school registers) taken by children in the different groups. Children of mothers who were at home had an average of 6.67 days absent over the 25 school weeks monitored; children whose mothers worked part-time took 5.35 days on average and children whose mothers worked fulltime took an average of only 3.00 days. This overall significant difference was made up of modest differences in both the number of episodes and the average duration of each episode.

We think that two factors might have contributed to the lack of difference seen in the retrospective data. When asked to recall an illness episode, there might have been a tendency for mothers to recall some types of episode rather than others. In addition, in this part of the study mothers were only asked about absence in a single illness episode and subtle differences between groups only really emerged when absences were added up over a period of time.

2. If children of working mothers have less absence, is this because they are attending school with colds, etc. which would lead to time off for children whose mothers are at home?

Although the groups differed on the amount of absence, there was no difference in the distribution of types of illness (coughs and colds, diarrhoea and vomiting, etc.) across children of full and part-time workers and mothers at home. Further, there seemed at first to be no clear evidence that working mothers adopted a different threshold of severity when deciding whether or not to keep their child off school. Using the best severity data, that on coughs and colds, there was no difference in the mean severity of episodes that had led to absence in the three groups.

One possible means of reconciling the different sets of findings was suggested from an inspection of the distributions of severity scores in the three groups. It was very noticeable that the range of severity scores exhibited by children of non-working mothers (6 to 105) was much higher than that seen in the children of fulltime workers (30 to 84); that is, some of the episodes seen in the former had been really very trivial, while others had been very serious respiratory conditions, often severe bouts of asthma. Formal statistical tests were carried out comparing the variability in the two groups and despite the relatively small number of episodes (n = 12) in the fulltime group, the result did approach statistical significance.

It seems likely that different explanations are required for the apparent shortfall of trivial and serious episodes in the children of fulltime workers. Mothers at home may have been more inclined to keep their children off school for trivial illnesses; and since episodes were identified in the study of school absence, trivial episodes that did not lead to absence would not have been detected. As for serious episodes, it is most unlikely that episodes generating scores in the sixties or above would not have led to school absence; so the most plausible explanation here is that mothers of children prone to such episodes, e.g. those with bad asthma, had decided they could not take on a fulltime job for that very reason. Both of these processes would contribute, via different chains of cause and effect, to reducing the overall amount of school absence in children of fulltime workers, while being consistent with no difference in the mean severity of illness episodes leading to absence in the different groups.

There was no evidence that any differences in management practices adopted by the two groups had any consequences for the children in terms of the duration or recurrence of illness episodes; but interpretation of such evidence would in any case not be straightforward, because of the different initial severity distributions that were found.

Part-time workers were omitted from the above analyses in order to facilitate the statistical comparisons. In terms of the distribution of severity scores, this group very much resembled the mothers at home and it may be that similar explanatory factors were involved.

3. Are there any differences in health service use, e.g. in the number of GP consultations?

The use made of health services did not differ between mothers who worked fulltime, part-time or those who were at home. The proportions of families consulting a GP were very similar (just under half) and across all groups, the mother was much the most likely person to accompany the child to the surgery. The pattern of diagnoses was the same across groups and there were no differences in the medication prescribed or bought.

For coughs and colds, where the most detailed severity data were available, there were no differences in the severity threshold for consulting across the groups, although within each group consulters had much higher severity scores than non-consulters.

In interpreting these findings, differences in the severity distributions need to be borne in mind: the higher proportion of very mild episodes in children whose mothers were at home might have suggested a lower rate of consultation (since severity is much the strongest predictor of consultation) in this group; but this might have been completely offset by a higher rate of consultation amongst parents of children with more severe disorders, also over-represented in the 'at home' group.

4. How dependent are working mothers on local kin, especially their own female relatives, for stand-in child health care?

From the retrospective data collected in the first phase of the study, it was clear that the problem of caring for ill children had to be seen in the context of providing routine child care and that the arrangements made by working mothers for out-of-hours and school holiday care were sometimes complicated and potentially fragile. To illustrate using holiday care, about a third of working mothers relied on grandparents (usually the mother's own mother) to provide some care during these periods, perhaps as part of a complicated rota involving a third carer as well as the mother herself. The working mothers described themselves as the main holiday carer in 58 of the 97 cases.

To remind readers of some local context here: of those women whose own mother was alive (81% of the sample), in 85% of cases she lived in or around Leeds. About half of the sample mothers saw their own mother several times a week and another quarter saw her at least once a week. Altogether, 111 of the 139 women in the sample (80%) claimed to be living near to members of their extended family.

Moving on to the prospective data and the ways in which illness episodes and school absence were managed by the families, in 238 out of 282 episodes, the mother claimed that she was the main carer. In the remaining 44 episodes, the main care was provided by fathers on eight occasions, grand-mothers 21, other relatives nine, paid helpers two and one other. In 92 episodes, a second person was involved in the care of the child. Overall, grandmothers were involved in care in 51 episodes (18%) and fathers in 35 (12%). In only 13 episodes was there any cash payment for help received.

Summarizing across episodes for each family, 63 of the mothers (57% of the 110 families in which there had been at least one illness episode) had relied on other people, either as primary or secondary carers, on at least one occasion. Thirty one of these mothers had relied on the child's grandparents (virtually always the maternal grandmother) for care on at least one occasion.

Simplifying the analysis by considering only the first illness episode, significant differences were found in the patterns of care provided by the different groups of families. In the families in which the mother was at home (and in which there had been an illness episode), the mother was the primary carer in 95% of cases; by comparison, in the families in which the mother was working, she was the primary carer in 79% of cases. Secondary carers other than the mother were involved in only 14% of families where the mother was at home, but in 33% of families where the mother was working. When it is remembered that illness episodes often began suddenly (see Point 2 above), it is clear how reliant mothers were on help from relatives being available sometimes at very short notice.

For fulltime workers, the mother's work absence was unrelated to whether or not her own mother lived nearby, but there was a strong relationship amongst part-time workers: these mothers were much more likely to have had work absence if the maternal grandmother did not live nearby.

5. What share of child health care is taken by the father?

Considering first their role in routine (i.e. non-illness) care, the Phase I data indicated that children's fathers played a very small part in care arrangements. To illustrate using holiday care, it was mentioned that 58 of the 97 working mothers (60%) said that they provided most of the care during school holidays. For the rest, the main carers comprised 17 grandparents, six paid babysitters, 13 other relatives, friends or neighbours and three fathers. Indeed, rather than being considered a resource for care, fathers were sometimes viewed as a handicap. The words of one lone parent bear repeating:

> You hear about some of these women . . . with children *and* a husband to look after. I don't know how they manage. We've just got ourselves to think about.

The position was very similar when the management of illness episodes was being considered. Out of 282 episodes, fathers were the main carers on eight occasions, mothers on 238. (The other carers are listed under Point 4 above.) Again, the words of one working mother convey the problem very well:

> I wasn't worried about the illness, she was just sick. My main worry was the fact that I would have to go to work, and what would I do? Well, her dad was moaning saying I wasn't very sympathetic, but I said, it is all right for you, you just go off to work, and it is me that is left wondering what on earth to do.

6. How important is child health care as a contributor to the absence from work figures of female employees?

Turning to mothers' work absence, in only 43 episodes (24% of the episodes occurring in the families of working mothers) did mothers need to take some time off work to care for their ill child. In a further eight episodes, they swapped shifts or made time up later. In 13 of these 51 episodes, less than a full work session was involved; 23 involved a full session, eight involved between one and two sessions and in only seven episodes (14%) was there more disturbance of work time than that.

Over the seven months covered by the study (which included the winter period when childhood illnesses are very much more common), the working mothers lost an average of 0.9 days each in order to care for ill health in the study's target child. When illness in non-study children was taken into account, this rose to 1.2 work days per mother.

Over the same period, the mothers took an average of 4.7 work days for their own sickness absence, although excluding three mothers who had very long absences reduced this figure to 2.1 days per mother. Additional leave for other family reasons, such as funerals or to cope with domestic emergencies such as the roof falling in, accounted for an additional 0.3 days per mother. Very approximately, therefore, child health care accounted for no more than a third of mothers' absence from work figures.

Only six fathers took time off work to care for an ill study child, four taking a half day, one a full day and one took 11 days – but that was only because the family was stranded abroad while on holiday. Twenty eight fathers took other very short absences for family reasons and 24 took sick leave; these two items together led to about 1.7 days of work absence per father.

7. What are the (perceived) reactions of employers to women's child health care responsibilities?

Because the UK has no statutory entitlement to leave for family reasons, it has been suggested that women commonly use 'the necessary lie' when their children are ill and claim sick leave on their own behalf. There was little support for this assertion in the present study data: in 35 of the 43 illness episodes where mothers took time off, they said that they had told their employers the truth. In other cases, the mother herself was ill and in only one instance did the mother admit to using the necessary lie. Of the 35 occasions when the mother said she was caring for an ill child, she lost pay on 20 of these and lost holiday time on nine more. Apart from a certain amount of disruption, therefore, employers bore the cost of childhood illness on only six occasions.

When mothers were asked in general terms about their employers' reactions to employees' health care responsibilities, these were often described as being unsympathetic. Mothers also perceived indirect costs:

> You can get compassionate leave from work, but I feel if I took that for her being ill, I would lose the chance of promotion. You are though as unreliable. I do know women who take compassionate leave for that, but I know what is said about them as I am near the manager's desk a lot.

This view constrasted somewhat with the reports mothers gave when they were asked about employers' reactions to actual illness episodes in their own child. In this context, the great majority of mothers expressed satisfaction with the reaction they had received. The two sets of findings are probably not as contradictory as appears at first. It is well established that women experience downward mobility when they return to work after having children and employers know that mothers are prepared to trade a certain amount of flexibility regarding child care against higher wage rates, chances of promotion, etc. Since employers actually bore very little of the costs of childhood illness in the present study, the bargain would seem to be quite an advantageous one from their point of view.

> If I get the results at work, they are not too bothered how I achieve it. The MD is very considerate ... the odd time I have taken time off he has been good about it. Provided I still sold the same amount, it does not matter.

8. To what extent is the economic burden of child health care shared among family members?

The costs of everyday care arrangements could be quite subtle. Only a few mothers paid cash for child care (six used childminders and one or two more paid for care from a relative) but many bought the carer presents of cigarettes, chocolates or flowers. Many took part in a direct exchange of services of some kind (e.g. wallpapering grandmother's bedroom) and indirect exchanges, as well as a general and sometimes very powerful sense of indebtedness, were also common.

When illness episodes arose, a similar barter arrangement often took place and it was relatively uncommon for money payment to be involved (see Point 4 above). Having entered into barter arrangements for child care, mothers were also usually faced with having to make up a swapped shift, or catch up on lost time or sales figures or whatever at work, since these kinds of arrangements were preferred to losing holidays or pay. When mothers did lose pay, this was reported to have caused them no real problems in only about a third of instances. It was not clear to what extent these financial problems were shared within the family or borne mainly by the mother. Mothers who lost holiday of course bore that cost themselves.

9. To what extent do difficulties in providing child health care contribute to increasing stress in working mothers?

Within our sample the overall level of psychological stress as measured by the General Health Questionnaire was higher than that found in other samples of employed people, but not as high as in the unemployed. There were no differences between full and part-time workers and mothers at home in terms of overall GHQ score. It was, however, found that anxiety scores were raised in fulltime workers who had had to take time off work to care for ill children, suggesting that difficulties in providing child health care make a specific contribution to stress levels in working mothers. Depressed mood, as other researchers have found, was more common in those mothers at home. The direction of cause and effect for this last mentioned relationship is particularly uncertain. It may be that being at home caused depression or it may be that women who are somewhat depressed are less likely to seek paid work. Both factors may operate to some extent. A study which followed women's mood and employment behaviour over a period of time would be necessary to shed further light on this issue.

IMPLICATIONS OF THE STUDY FINDINGS

The over-riding conclusion emerging from our study is that in sickness and in health, the juggling act of combining work and family responsibilities is a solo act. It is performed, within any one family, by the mother with some assistance from her female relatives. Fathers play a comparatively minor part. Further, the costs of the juggling act are borne almost entirely by mothers, rather than being shared with other family members. A critic could of course argue that in a general sense we knew all that already but it is not in a general sense that our study data are compelling. What they convey is the scale of the problem – the sheer weight of the task that mothers are taking on and being increasingly obliged to take on.

Taking a different tack, a critic could accept the facts, but point out that women freely choose to engage in paid work and know in some sense what they are letting themselves in for. Problems that arise are therefore their problems and not a matter for society or for policy makers. In what sense is this true? To what extent are mothers solving other people's problems for them – carrying other people's costs?

Mothers, as far as we could tell, went to a great deal of trouble to provide the best possible care for their children, both routinely and during episodes of childhood illness. The management of the illnesses themselves – GP consultations and so on – did not differ in any material way between working and non-working mothers and we found no evidence to suggest that the health of children was being adversely affected by mothers' employment obligations. The mothers tried very hard, in other words, to prevent their children having to carry any kind of cost. The mothers provided most of the child care themselves and when this was not possible, substitute care from known and trusted others was somehow arranged. The maternal grandmother played an important part in these arrangements. In a variety of ways, mothers sought to recompense substitute carers for their time and trouble.

No-one would argue that children or grandparents should carry a greater share of the costs of the juggling act. But what about fathers? In our study, fathers contributed very little to the care of their children, in sickness or in health. What about employers? Mothers did not expect them to carry costs and apart from a certain amount of disruption caused by absence, the costs were indeed passed on from employer to employee: shifts were swapped, time was made up, holidays and pay were sacrificed. Employers were usually perceived as being sympathetic to employees taking time off work to care for ill children and were rewarded with the mother's gratitude in consequence. 'Sympathetic' in this context almost always meant that no additional penalty was exacted over and beyond docked pay or lost holidays. Even that could be misleading, as employers' sympathy was often part of an implicit pact with mothers, in which pay rates, promotion prospects and other conditions of service were traded for the 'flexibility' which working mothers required.

THE LONGER TERM

The main focus of this book is child health care. From the above, however, it is clear that the main implications of our findings are not for health care directly; working mothers are already providing the health care that their children need. The main implications are indirect and relate to how mothers can be helped to provide child care, including child health care, at less cost to themselves.

In the UK, policy makers tend to regard such matters as their business only when certain conditions prevail in the economy. If the economy is expanding, as it was in the mid-1980s, then attention begins to be paid to the problems of women workers and policy changes to encourage mothers back into the labour force begin to be discussed. If the economy takes a downturn, as has happened more recently, such items rapidly lose their place on the political agenda.

Economic management in the UK has often been accused of 'short-termism', in which immediate benefits are characteristically chosen in preference to longer term investment. The employer who prefers not to hire women, especially mothers, because they are 'unreliable' is looking at the perceived short term cost but ignoring the potential long term benefits flowing from increasing the pool of talent available to the organization. The employer who capitalizes on the rules regarding part-time employment and hires mothers as part-time workers with few rights and few prospects is also acting in the short term interests of his or her organization. This practice is actively encouraged by the current government, who see it as an admirable way of keeping down business costs. The long term costs to the economy of moving ever further down this road are not included in the calculation. Employers are encouraged to choose their employees from a reduced pool of talent and much of the investment that has already been made educating and training women on a more or less equal footing with men is wasted if the majority of them are consigned by other forces to a low wage, low skill economy. It would of course cause furore to propose that women should not receive education and training on the same footing as men but no furore at all is caused by documenting the extent to which that investment is wasted.

As was pointed out in Chapter 1, there are countries which do things differently. The whole thrust of EEC social and economic policy is based on a much more long term view of managing human resources but the UK government has explicitly rejected this approach by rejecting the Social Chapter of the Maastricht Treaty. In the Scandinavian countries, Sweden in particular, child care is regarded as an investment, improving the efficiency of the labour market and hence of the economy as a whole.

One aspect of the EEC policy and Swedish practice of particular relevance to child health care is the issue of family leave. After an extensive data gathering exercise and lengthy discussions, the European Childcare Network recommended that 'There should be leave for family reasons, to enable parents to take time off work to undertake essential parental duties, including the care of sick children'. This leave should be 'equally available to men and women . . . linked to benefit payments from public funds . . . (and) available to all employees' (Phillips and Moss, 1988). Since that time, the European Commission has adopted a non-binding Recommendation which asks member states to develop measures in a number of areas, including family leave.

Given the hostility which such proposals arouse in UK government circles, the experience of Sweden is highly instructive. Sweden introduced a family leave provision in 1974, long enough ago for its working to be monitored. The leave entitlement stood for several years at 60 days per child per year and in some circumstances 90 days are now possible. In a recent article comparing Swedish and UK experiences, Bronwen Cohen (1991) wrote:

> With over half of Swedish parents using five benefit days or less and over three quarters using ten or fewer days, it is evident that allowing a generous leave entitlement does not mean parents permanently stay away from work.

Analysing the Swedish data by age of child suggests an age related entitlement might be feasible, with parents of a 5–8 year-old qualifying for eight days leave per annum.

Our own study data are relevant here. Over the seven months covered by the study, which included the winter period when illnesses are common, the working mothers reported taking an average of 1.5 days off work for what could be described as family reasons. Even scaled up to a full year, these figures are obviously lower than the Swedish ones. Our study mothers might have been under-reporting to some extent, but it also seems likely that the cost to them of taking time off work was so high that they kept their absence to the absolute minimum. Swedish mothers (and fathers) had more of a choice, which they obviously exercised very responsibly, given the amount of leave they actually took compared to the 60 days allowed at the time.

Elsewhere in her paper, Cohen (1991) reports on two surveys by the Institute of Personnel Management. These show that in the United Kingdom, where family leave is at the discretion of employers, managers are *less* likely to grant leave for family problems now than they were ten years ago. The family problems do not of course go away as a result of these policies; they show up instead in the absence from work statistics. Drawing on a number of sources, including the government sponsored General Household Survey (GHS), Cohen summarizes as follows:

Men with a youngest dependent child over 5 have the same absence rate for personal and other reasons as men without dependent children. Absence rates for women with a youngest dependent child over 5 drop significantly (i.e. compared to under-5s) but are still twice as high as for women without dependent children.

In another analysis of GHS data, Arber (1990) looked at sickness absence and reported that;

Contrary to popular opinion, women with dependent children are no more likely to be away from work because of illness than women without children.

She also found that women who worked fulltime had on average ten days sickness absence per year compared with nine days for men, a difference which was very substantially smaller than had previously been supposed.

Employers' arguments that women, and especially mothers, are 'unreliable' workers need to be re-examined in the context of these findings. Women's own sickness absence is not very much worse than that of men and their absence for family reasons, including the care of sick children, probably amounts to no more than a few days a year.

A family leave entitlement of about eight days a year, which could be taken in part days as necessary, would make an enormous difference to the lives of working mothers in this country. As with most other child care initiatives, it would make economic as well as social sense. Other changes might also follow: in Sweden, an increasing number of men are taking family leave days, suggesting that legitimizing the provision of family leave by locating it within the rest of the National Insurance and social benefit system can eventually lead to a change in attitudes and even a change in behaviour.

The present UK government is most unlikely to introduce a system of family leave unless the EEC somehow manages to force them into it. The other set of changes which would greatly help working women is also being resisted: these relate to restrictions on the number of hours in a working week. If men were to do fewer hours at work and more hours at home, this would increase and improve the opportunities for women. Unfortunately, the prevailing culture of British management demands the opposite, with a ten or 12-hour day being required of anyone who wants to climb the career ladder. In Germany, according to McGwire (1991), a manager who works more than a 40-hour week is considered to be inefficient rather than dedicated.

It is too much to expect male managers and male employees to change current practices of their own accord: in the present culture, a male employee who insists on leaving work at 5pm or 5.30pm to share in looking after his family would be regarded as 'not one of us' and treated accordingly. A change in the law to legitimize leaving at 5.30pm for both males and females might therefore help women workers indirectly as well as directly.

A blurring of the boundaries between part-time and fulltime work would also help. Many women do want to work part-time while their children are young; in the UK that means accepting poorer pay and conditions of services. In a recent court case, the Equal Opportunities Commission argued that this constituted indirect sex discrimination, since 90% of part-time workers in the UK are women. The case was lost on the grounds that improving conditions would place an increased burden on employers, which would lead in turn to a loss of employment opportunities for women. The Secretary of State for Employment's concern about the risk to employment opportunities for women throughout the country 'could not be equated with a policy that they should be treated as cheap labour' (*Guardian*, 16.10.91). Again, other countries do things differently and cause and effect is unlikely to be as simple as the Employment Secretary claims.

On a more positive note, a few things are changing in the right direction. Out-of-school care is at last being recognized as a problem area, with some Department of Employment money being directed into it via Training and Enterprise Councils and charities such as the Kids Club Network.

Opportunity 2000 is trying to increase the number of women in senior management positions, which might eventually change some of the worst aspects of macho management culture and have a 'trickle down' effect for ordinary working women. That said, a lot of the rhetoric about barriers to women's progress dwells on things like confidence rather than 12-hour days or the decreasing availability of time off work for family reasons. It also again presupposes that it is the women who have to do the accommodating to the demands of work rather than the other way around.

The women in our study already squeezed an enormous amount of productive activity into their day. The penalties they earned were for spreading their energies across different types of productive activity, rather than concentrating them on paid work as men do. It is obvious that the answer cannot be for women to adopt the male pattern, even if they wanted to – which on the whole they do not. The current male pattern is entirely reliant on women not devoting all their time and energies to their jobs; as others have pointed out (Moss and Fonda, 80), working mothers are not 'the problem'. The problem lies in society's failure to develop structures which allow the roles of worker and parent to be combined without penalizing the people involved.

It is important and right that statements of aims should be phrased in neutral terms: structures are needed which do not penalize 'people'. It is also important not to forget that most of the people currently being penalized are women. Again, this can be read as a statement of the obvious. There are many male managers who acknowledge that their 14-hour working day could not be sustained without the support of their wife. They accept too that this may have entailed career sacrifices on the wife's behalf. 'But', they say, 'my wife and I made the choices that were best for us. It just made sense for *us*.' Framing the decision in terms of personal choice like this has the effect of implying they could just as well have chosen some other set of arrangements. Some people choose this way, some people choose that. It is but a short step from here to the implication that the support system upon which they rely is equally available to everybody and all people have to do is choose to arrange their affairs in that way. Within this framework of beliefs and assumptions, managers can maintain that they treat all their employees equally and deny that it is in any way discriminatory to withdraw support for family leave or extend the working day in the morning or evening or in other ways inflict penalties differentially on their female employees. If everybody has the same choices and the same opportunities to get the necessary support system organized, then it is the individual's responsibility if their personal support system is not up to scratch.

What we are witnessing is not a large number of personal choices that happen to be this way but could just have well have been that. It is not a statistical accident that most of 'the people' currently being penalized by trying to combine the roles of worker and parent are women. Women and men do not have the same choices and the same opportunities; they do not have the same access to the personal support system that a wife traditionally provides. Against this backcloth, equality of treatment at work is anything but equality of opportunity.

Numerous studies in the UK and elsewhere (e.g. Witherspoon, 1988) have shown that domestic workload is shared very unequally between women and men, whether or not the women have paid work. Our own study adds to and extends this literature into the field of child health care. Not only do women lack the support system that men have, the lack counts double because they spend a lot of time providing a support system for somebody else. The findings of a recent study in Sweden are illuminating, if somewhat depressing (Frankenhaeuser *et al.*, 1990). The study was about the 'total workload' of men and women, which included housework and child care as well as paid work.

The present data show that women employed fulltime have a total workload of 78 hours per week compared with 68 hours for men. In other words, men have about two hours more free time per workday than women. In families with three or four children as well as in families with young children, the difference between men's and women's work week increases . .

It is noteworthy that it is not only in terms of hours of work that women carry the heaviest load. They also have the main responsibility for most duties in the household as well as for child care. Thus, insofar as employed women suffer from work overload, this is likely to be due to the unpaid work.

The authors noted that a similar American study had produced almost identical figures – 68 hours for men and 80 hours for women. Back in the UK, a 1992 report from the Henley Centre (which produces reports for business on consumer attitudes and behaviour) remorselessly documents how much more shopping, cleaning and child care women do than men, but also includes the survey finding that 77% of UK men agree with the statement, 'Men should share more of the everyday household chores'.

Improving institutional arrangements – family leave, child care and so on – is necessary but, as the Swedish experience shows, not sufficient. Improving attitudes, as the Henley study shows, is only a first step. It is behaviour which must change and that is a very slow process.

The mothers in our study may not have read the academic literature on women's employment, but they had a pretty realistic idea of the amount of support they could expect from their husbands and partners. They also attached high value to being good mothers – as most mothers do. The end product was a pretty realistic idea of the kinds of jobs and work arrangements that were open to them, i.e. consistent with their values but also with their expectations of support. Satisfaction was then a function of the extent to which their job expectations had been met.

All recent surveys (e.g. Witherspoon and Prior, 1991) show that part-time working is attractive to mothers of young children and our study findings do not contradict this. Mothers' genuine desire to spend time in the company of their children should not, however, be regarded as a justification for all the injustices of the status quo. Many mothers in our study would have changed their work patterns if an adequate support system had been available. Hardly anybody would 'prefer' – if that word carries any meaning at all – to find themselves in the predicament described below. The quotation is from an interview with a mother in our sample who worked nights as an auxiliary nurse. She had accepted poor working conditions in exchange for an informal arrangement with her employer which enabled her to take her children into work during illness episodes.

> In other countries parents get time off, you don't here. I think you should. In this country you are just expected to cope. If you are a woman and you have to go out to work you are a second class citizen. It is not like a man going out to work. I trained for three years, but because I have children I am not expected to reach my full potential. I have spent the last 13 years doing menial jobs. It used to be that my mum would help me out, but she died about nine months ago. I have found out how hard it is since. 24 hours looking after children and no help. [At work] we are all part-timers, they wouldn't pay single women these wages. [My employer] uses us and we use her – we get these low wages because of this.

Again, we must acknowledge that many people see nothing objectionable in all this. The Social Chapter of the Maastricht Treaty might have begun to iron out some of the grosser inequalities between workers, but the UK government argues that the Chapter will place too heavy a burden on employers and will not accept it. Wages Councils are being abolished for the same reason. In an earlier part of this chapter, we discussed some of the long term costs to the economy that this approach entails.

And the costs to the women themselves? It has been a theme throughout this book that the costs of 'the juggling act' – reconciling work and family responsibilities – are almost entirely borne by women. Because the costs are so pervasive and change women's lives so much, a little curiosity is justified regarding the longer term consequences of arranging our affairs in this way. Bluntly put, one consequence might be that more and more women will see the writing on the wall and decide to have fewer children or not to have any at all. The number of babies born in Europe is currently only three quarters of that needed to maintain existing levels of population and a falling population is predicted between now and 2020 (Family Policy Studies Centre, 1991). In Sweden, by contrast, where it is easier to combine work and parenthood, the birthrate has steadily increased since the mid-1980s and is now at replacement level.

The divorce rate in the UK is high and rising: more than one new marriage in three now ends in divorce. The increasing number of single parent families is a drain on the Social Security budget. By mentioning these facts, we are not of course suggesting that there is a one-to-one causal relationship between the problems experienced by working mothers and the high rate of family breakdown – but neither do we believe that the mothers' problems are irrelevant. Male partners were not a very conspicuous asset for many of the women in our study and some women even considered them a liability. No doubt some of the men felt they were being short-changed as their wives honoured obligations to children, relatives, schools and employers. It may be that at times of particular stress, the grass on the other side of the matrimonial fence seems particularly green.

The mothers in our study did not expect miracles. To them, the child care and family policy that operates in Sweden would sound like an impossible dream. In the UK, the reality is that the lack of formal support leaves the working mother of a sick child in a 'no win' situation. Either she patches together some form of substitute child care while she works or she negotiates time off work to care for her child herself. Neither arrangement might be satisfactory to the mother and she may experience guilt on either count.

The final irony is that until official and personal attitudes change towards working mothers, the women who bear the costs and make the sacrifices needed to perform 'the juggling act' still tend to be regarded by male employers and colleagues as 'skiving' or 'taking advantage'. The words of one of the working mothers in our study deserve repeating:

It would be wonderful to have time off and people don't frown about it . . . and not to feel guilty . . . and your work colleagues wouldn't think you were skiving – especially the men.

References

Abrams, P., Abrams, S., Humphrey, R. and Snaith, R. (1989) *Neighbourhood Care and Social Policy*, HMSO, London.

Arber, S. (1990) Revealing women's health: re-analysing the General Household Survey, in *Women's Health Counts*, (ed. H. Roberts), Routledge, London.

Banks, M.H., Clegg, C.W., Jackson, P.R. *et al*. (1980) The use of the General Health Questionnaire as an indicator of mental health in occupational studies. *Journal of Occupational Psychology*, **53**, 187–94.

Bartley, M., Popay, J. and Plewis, I. (1992) Domestic conditions, paid employment and women's experience of ill-health. *Sociology of Health and Illness*, **14**(3), 313–43.

Brannen, J. (1989) Childbirth and occupational mobility: evidence from a longitudinal study. *Work, Employment and Society*, **3**, 179–201.

Brannen, J. and Moss, P. (1988) *New Mothers at Work: Employment and Childcare*, Unwin, London.

Brannen, J. and Moss, P. (1990) *Managing Mothers: Dual Earner Households after Maternity Leave*, Unwin Hyman, London.

Brown, G.W. and Harris, T.O. (1978) *Social Origins of Depression*, Tavistock, London.

Campbell, J.D. (1978) The child in the sick role: contributions of age, sex, parental status and parental values. *Journal of Health and Social Behaviour*, **19**, 35–51.

Campion, P.D. and Gabriel, J. (1984) Child consultation patterns in general practice: comparing 'high' and 'low' consulting families. *British Medical Journal*, **288**, 1426–8.

CEC (Commission of the European Communities), Directorate-General for Employment, Industrial Relations and Social Affairs (1990) *Employment in Europe*, Office of Official Publications of the European Communities, Luxembourg.

Clarke, A. and Hewison, J. (1991) Whether or not to consult a general practitioner: decision making by parents in a multi-ethnic inner-city area, in *Child Health Matters*, (eds S. Wyke and J. Hewison), Open University Press, Milton Keynes.

Cohen, B. (1991) Taking time off: leave provision in the European Community for parents of school-age children. *Women's Studies International Forum*, **14(6)**, 585–98.

Cohen, B. and Fraser, N. (1991) *Childcare in a Modern Welfare System*, Institute for Public Policy Research, London.

Dex, S. (1988) *Women's Attitudes Towards Work*, Macmillan, Basingstoke.

Equal Opportunities Commission (1990) *The Key to Real Choice and Action Plan for Child Care*, EOC, Manchester.

Equal Opportunities Commission (1992) *Women's Employment: Britain in the Single European Market*, EOC, Manchester.

Family Policy Studies Centre (1991) *August Bulletin*, FPSC, London.

Finch, J. and Groves, D. (eds) (1983) *A Labour of Love: Women, Work and Caring*, Routledge and Kegan Paul, London.

Frankenhaeuser, M., Lundberg, U. and Mardberg, B. (1990) *The Total Workload of Men and Women as Related to Occupational Level and Number and Age of Children*. Report from the Department of Psychology, Stockholm University, No. 726.

Goldberg, D.P. and Williams, P. (1988) *A User's Guide to the General Health Questionnaire*, NFER-Nelson, Windsor.

Guardian Law Reports (1991) Treatment of part-timers is justified. *Guardian*, 16th October.

Handy, C. (1978) Going against the grain: working couples and greedy occupations, in *Working Couples* (eds R. Rapoport, R. Rapoport and J. Bumstead), Routledge and Kegan Paul, London.

Hannay, D.R. (1979) *The Symptom Iceberg: A Study of Community Health*, Routledge and Kegan Paul, London.

Helman, C. (1990) *Culture, Health and Illness*, 2nd edn, Wright, Bristol.

Henley Centre (1992) *Planning for Consumer Change in Europe*, Henley Centre for Forecasting and Research International, London.

Isaacs, D. (1987) Why do children get colds? in *Progress in Child Health*, *Vol. 3*, (ed. J.A. MacFarlane), Churchill Livingstone, Edinburgh.

Joshi, J. (1987) The cost of caring, in *Women and Poverty in Britain*, (eds B. Glendinning and J. Miller), Harvester Press, Brighton.

Lau, B.W.K. (1987) Trivia in general practice. *Practitioner*, **231**, 1333–5.

Levene, H. (1960) Robust tests for the equality of variance, in *Contributions to Probability and Statistics*, (ed I. Olkin), Stanford University Press, Palo Alto, CA.

Lewis, S.N. and Cooper, C.L. (1987) Stress in two-earner couples and stage in the life cycle. *Journal of Occupational Psychology*, **60**, 289–303.

Ley, P. (1988) *Communicating with Patients*, Chapman & Hall, London.

Mayall, B. (1986) *Keeping Children Healthy*, Allen and Unwin, London.

McGwire, S. (1991) Victims of the macho culture. *Guardian*, 29th October.

Melhuish, C.E. and Moss, P. (eds) (1991) *Day Care for Young Children: International Perspectives*, Routledge, London.

Moss, P., Bolland, G., Foxman, R. and Owen, (1987) The division of household work during the transition to parenthood. *Journal of Reproductive and Infant Psychology*, 5, 71–86.

Moss, P. and Fonda, N. (eds) (1980) *Work and the Family*, Temple Smith, London.

North of England Study of Standards and Performance in General Practice (1990) *The Effects of Setting and Implementing Clinical Standards*, Health Care Research Unit Report No. 42, University of Newcastle upon Tyne.

OPCS Monitor (1992) *General Household Survey 1991*, Office of Population Censuses and Surveys, London.

Petrie, P. and Logan, P. (1986) *After School and in the Holidays: The Responsibility for Looking after School Children*, Thomas Coram Research Unit Working and Occasional Papers No. 2, Institute of Education, University of London.

Phillips, A. and Moss, P. (1988) *Who Cares for Europe's Children? The Short Report of the European Childcare Network*, Commission of the European Communities, Brussels.

Presser, H.B. (1989) Some economic complexities of child care provided by grandmothers. *Journal of Marriage and the Family*, 51, 581–91.

Prout, A. (1988) Off school sick: mothers' accounts of school sickness absence. *The Sociological Review*, 36(4). 765–89.

Rapoport, R., Rapoport, R. and Bumstead, J. (eds) (1978) *Working Couples*, Routledge and Kegan Paul, London.

Ross, C.E. and Mirowsky, J. (1988) Child care and emotional adjustment to wives' employment. *Journal of Health and Social Behaviour*, 29, 127–38.

Royal College of General Practitioners (1986) *Morbidity Statistics from General Practice 1981–2: Third National Study*, Office of Population Censuses and Surveys/Department of Health and Social Security/HMSO, London.

Spencer, N.J. (1984) Parents' recognition of their ill child, in *Progress in Child Health, Vol. 1*, (ed. J.A. MacFarlane), Churchill Livingstone, Edinburgh.

Voydanoff, P. and Donnelly, B.W. (1989) Work and family roles and psychological distress. *Journal of Marriage and the Family*, 51, 923–32.

Walby, S. and Bagguley, P. (1990) Sex segregation in local labour markets. *Work, Employment and Society*, 4, 59–81.

Witherspoon, S. (1988) Interim Report: a woman's work, in *British Social Attitudes: the 5th Report*, (eds R. Jowell, S. Witherspoon and L. Brook), Gower, Aldershot.

Witherspoon, S. and Prior, G. (1991) Working mothers: free to choose? in *British Social Attitudes: the 8th Report*, (eds R. Jowell, L. Brook and B. Taylor), Gower, Aldershot, pp. 131–54.

Wyke, S. and Hewison, J. (eds) (1991) *Child Health Matters*, Open University Press, Milton Keynes.

Wyke, S., Hewison, J., Hey, E.N. and Russell, I.T. (1991) Respiratory illness in children: do deprived children have worse coughs? *Acta Paediatrica Scandinavica*, **80**, 704–11.

Wyke, S., Hewison, J. and Russell, I.T. (1990) Respiratory illness in children: who consults the doctor? *British Journal of General Practice*, **40**, 226–9.

Index